D0586244

Why Can't I Ever Be Good Enough?

Escaping the Limits
of Your Childhood Roles

JOAN RUBIN-DEUTSCH, LICSW

NEW HARBINGER PUBLICATIONS, INC.

Publisher's Note

This publication is designed to provide accurate and authoritative information in regard to the subject matter covered. It is sold with the understanding that the publisher is not engaged in rendering psychological, financial, legal, or other professional services. If expert assistance or counseling is needed, the services of a competent professional should be sought.

Distributed in the U.S.A. by Publishers Group West; in Canada by Raincoat Books; in Great Britain by Hi Marketing, Ltd.; in South Africa by Real Books, Ltd.; in Australia by Boobook; and in New Zealand by Tandem Press.

Copyright © 2003 by Joan Rubin-Deutsch
New Harbinger Publications, Inc.
5674 Shattuck Avenue
Oakland, CA 94609

Cover design by Salmon Studios
Cover image by Greg Ceo/Getty Images
Edited by Wendy Millstine
Text design by Tracy Marie Carlson

ISBN 1-57224-314-7 Paperback

All Rights Reserved

Printed in the United States of America

New Harbinger Publications' Web site address: www.newharbinger.com

05   04   03

10   9   8   7   6   5   4   3   2   1

First printing

This book is dedicated to my father, Harold Rubin. Though his time with me on this earth was much too brief, I always knew I was cherished and valued. The legacy of love he left has allowed me to break free from unhealthy internal contracts and enter into healthy ones that enrich my spirit.

Contents

A thank-you to the following people for contributing to the richness in my life:

My husband, Owen, whose love and support ground me in every way. My amazing and beautiful daughter, Elizabeth, who constantly expands my heart. My brother, Robert Gruberman, for the loving connection we share. Greta Rittenburg, for mentoring me and planting the seeds for this book. Cynthia King and Mari LaPage, extraordinary healers and guides. Dear friends Szifra Birke, Judi Watson, and Maxine Zarchan, who always believed in me. Jueli Gastwirth, Senior Acquisitions Editor at New Harbinger and kindred spirit. And every client I have ever worked with who entrusted me with their most vulnerable self.

Chapter 1

Listening

Discovering

When you were a child, you relied on your parents to nurture and take care of you. They gave you messages, explicit or implicit, about what they expected from you. Because you wanted and needed their love and approval, you did your best to comply with their expectations.

If family messages were healthy, clear, and consistent, you learned you could trust your parents. They said what they meant and they meant what they said. This allowed you to feel emotionally safe and comfortable. You knew what was expected from you. There were appropriate boundaries and limits set. You understood the rules. If you were listened to and treated with respect, you were able to express your thoughts and feelings without fear of recrimination. If you were told you were special and valued, you were able to internalize the message that you were both loved and loveable. As an adult, it is likely that you have good self-esteem and are comfortable with who you are. You are able to develop and maintain solid, caring relationships.

If family messages were unhealthy, unclear, and inconsistent, you learned just the opposite. You couldn't trust your parents to follow through with what they said and you never knew what the rules and expectations were. Your home environment was filled with tension and stress. *You* were filled with tension and stress. You were not taught that you were special and valued as the child you were. Rather, you learned to be very careful about what you said and how you behaved. What you internalized was a fear that you were not good enough and not deserving of love.

As an adult, you question all your thoughts and feelings and are uncomfortable with who you are. Your relationships suffer because you have difficulty believing you are worthy of being loved. You are confused about what you need and what you want. Your life is not working for you, even though you keep trying to make it better. You keep repeating the same unhealthy patterns, making the same mistakes, and experiencing the same failures. If you knew how to do things differently, you would.

If you have been deeply wounded as a result of your childhood experiences, healing from these wounds is a journey you can now decide to embark on. The focus of this book is on helping you to understand how you have gotten caught up in negative patterns and themes and teaching you ways to break through them. You will come to understand that you no longer need to comply with someone else's definition or perception of who you are or must be. You can be the person *you* choose to be. You will discover that you are special, valuable, and worthy of being loved. As a result, your relationships with others will become healthier. You can create a life that has meaning, purpose, comfort, and serenity. You will do this by identifying the unhealthy childhood contracts that you have entered into, finding out how to break them, and learning to rewrite them.

What Is a Contract?

A contract, in a literal sense, is a binding agreement between two parties. The agreement is oral or written. This agreement is mutual and the terms of the contract require you to do or perform a specified set of tasks. In return, you will receive something that is of value to you.

In this book, I refer to a "contract" as an internal process. When you were a child, you weighed and measured whatever reactions and responses you received from your family, and formulated an idea of what you needed to do in order to get your needs met. In this context, I will explore the concept of a contract as a binding agreement that you made in your childhood with yourself, though you *believed* there was a mutual agreement between you and your parents. This contract became an organizing principle that determined how you would operate in your family and later, in the outside world.

Taking Back Your Power

When you entered into your internal contracts, you unknowingly gave some or all of your personal power away. When you were little, your parents were in control. They needed to be so that they could provide for your emotional and physical well-being. It was also important that they accepted and welcomed your independent thoughts and feelings. If they didn't do this, you never developed the capacity to believe that your thoughts and feelings were valid. You felt powerless. In your adult relationships, you have either relinquished your power or you have tried to control everyone and everything. If you look at your love relationships, what do you see? Who has the power? If you look at your relationships with your children, who is in control? Are you still struggling with your parents? What about your work relationships? Your friendships? Are you able to speak up and express your thoughts, needs, wishes, desires? Are you able to negotiate differences?

Whether you are giving your power away, or needing to be in control, the bottom line is the same. Inside, you really feel powerless. Maybe it's time to learn that you no longer have to give away your power in order to have what you want and deserve. Maybe it's time to learn how to release painful thoughts, feelings, and connections to the past that limit you. Maybe it's time to learn how to envision and create the life you want to be living. If not now, when? How long do you want to spend your life conforming to the needs and demands of everyone else and denying yourself? How long do you want to feel angry and resentful because no one is listening to you and no one is respectful of who you are? Are you aware of how much energy it takes to constantly give yourself away to others instead of taking care of yourself first?

Everything you need to know is inside of you. Through discussion and exercises, you will be given information that will allow you to discover that who you really are is acceptable and that what you really want is valid. You will be given tools and skills that will enable you to release the wounds that have kept you locked inside your doubts and fears.

What This Book Will Teach You

This book is about how the messages you received in childhood evolved into binding contracts. These contracts became mind-sets that influenced the way you have thought, felt, and behaved to this point. By reading this book, you will learn:

* How to release painful connections to the past that limit you.

* To *listen* to and distinguish your own inner voice from the other internalized critical voices you carry within.

* How to develop and maintain a conscious awareness of your thoughts, feelings, and behaviors.

* Why you react to unresolved emotional issues and how to respond instead.

* How your contracts influence the way you connect and disconnect in relationships.

* How to deepen and expand your relationships.

* How to build a healthier sense of self.

* Skills to envision and create the life you want to be living.

How to Use This Book

This book offers a step-by-step guide to healing from a painful childhood. Each section builds onto the prior section. In presenting the material in this way, you will be able to understand and experience healing as a focused process. You will be an active participant in your own evolution. It is best to do the work beginning with chapter 1 and in segments because you will need time to absorb the concepts, practice the meditations, review the answers to questions, and integrate your learning. You may need more time to do some chapters than others. The work is challenging but hopefully, it will also be a thoughtful, meaningful, and growth-enhancing experience for you.

Wake-Up Calls

Awakening is the first step toward the process of change. Until you become attuned to your negative patterns and themes, you will continue to repeat them.

My own personal awakening began several years ago. I believed I was attentive to my thoughts and feelings, needs and wishes. I took time for myself, and I appreciated my family, friends, and work. I felt fulfilled in all aspects of my life and was grateful. And then I became very ill and my life came to a halt. I asked the question I always ask when life takes a turn. What is this supposed to be teaching me? And I listened, really listened over a period of weeks and months.

As a result, I learned, and am still learning, about myself. There were so many singular and global truths that I had not been paying attention to. It was a stunning experience. I thought I knew most things about myself, about my impact on my world and about the world's impact on me. I had spent so much of my life paying attention, yet I had indeed missed some major truths and now I was getting a wake-up call. Something had to change. What about you? Are you getting messages that are letting you know that you need to do things differently? Are you ready to listen to your wake-up calls?

Wake-up calls will tap you on the shoulder, quietly at first, then more and more insistently if you ignore them. Awakening to the realization that your life is not on track, is not feeling good to you, and opening to the possibility that things can be different is the beginning of change. It really is possible to create a life that feels physically, emotionally, psychologically, and spiritually healthy. It really is possible to have a life that is filled with loving connections. Taking care of yourself first will bring you these things.

Taking Care of Yourself First

Before you can be there for anyone else, you must learn to be present for your own self. When I became ill, my diagnosis was that I was having a toxic allergic reaction to something, but the doctors couldn't figure out what that something was. I firmly believed that I had become allergic to my life. I had spent many years learning and teaching the mind/body connection. I knew that our thoughts and feelings are intertwined. I knew that when we hold in emotional pain, it finds alternate pathways through the body. I, as the teacher, was now the student teaching myself what I thought I already understood on all levels.

Along with an intense work schedule, I was experiencing many personal losses. My daughter was growing up and away. While I supported her being independent, I missed her terribly. Additionally, there were painful family events taking place that I could not control. My family extended to my clients. I mothered them all. I provided a safety net for them. I loved them, believed in them, accepted them, comforted them, and taught them how to love themselves. As the intensity of the work increased, I gave more of myself.

When I became too ill to work, I had to give myself a reprieve. Getting through the day became my only focus. I became aware of my own voice telling me I needed time to retreat. I experienced a huge sense of relief at this concept. I had an epiphany. I didn't have to take care of everyone. I only had to focus on myself. I now gave myself permission to just be. I began to understand the organizing principle that had influenced my life path. I began to clearly see that I had made a number of childhood contracts, one of which was to be a caregiver. If I did this well, I would receive the approval and applause I thought I needed. While I did receive the approval and applause, I also suffered the consequences. I was physically, emotionally, and spiritually depleted. I was no longer experiencing joy in my life. I now had to really integrate the concept that I taught so well. It's not only okay, but it's healthy to take care of yourself first. It is not selfish. It is self-caring and it is life enhancing. What about you? Do you take care of yourself first?

Do you:

* Tend to put others' needs before your needs?

* Say yes to requests when you really feel no?

* Have difficulty setting limits with your own physical and emotional endurance?

* Hold feelings in so that you either get depressed or explode in an angry outburst?

* Experience physical symptoms such as headaches, backaches, or stomach upsets frequently?

* Have difficulty identifying and/or asking for what you need?

* Often feel that no one understands or cares about your needs?

* Settle for less than you think you deserve?

If you answered yes to a majority of these questions, you are a person who is not putting yourself first. This is your opportunity to begin to open to the concept that you are deserving and your needs are important.

Learning to Listen to Your Needs

Listening to your needs and taking good care of yourself nurture you. If you ignore your needs, there will be a price to pay. You cannot go through life unconsciously and without consequences. Every living thing requires attention in order to flourish. What happens when you ignore your plants? They dry up. What happens when you give them plant food and water them regularly? They blossom. You need and deserve attention so that you can blossom and flourish.

When I was ill, I felt that I had no control of my body or my life. At first, I was so sick and so weak that most of my thoughts were fearful. I was afraid of dying, afraid of having tests and procedures, afraid I would never recover, afraid I would be alone, afraid to be alone, afraid to drive, afraid to go for a walk by myself. I hated that I felt so sick and I hated that I was so afraid. I needed to find a way to intercept this debilitating process. I decided to honor my body and my feelings and to listen carefully to what I needed. I became more in touch with bodily sensations. I became able to hear different parts of my body "speaking" to me. If I heard "rest," I rested. If it was "eat," I'd eat. If I heard "sleep," I'd sleep. One day, I heard it telling me that my diet was wrong for me and that I was having reactions to foods I was eating. I did some research, bought books on food allergies, and then began to feel better.

It became clearer and clearer that I did not want to be working so hard, seeing so many clients, carrying all that pain. As much as I would try, I was unable to block all the energy that came toward me in sessions. The way I worked was antithetical to this notion. "Feeling" clients was how I connected to them and how I knew what they were struggling with emotionally and even where in their bodies they were holding their pain. The options available to me were: (1) to stop doing clinical work, which was not really an option for me because I loved my work, or (2) to cut back on the hours I would work. While this seemed the most appropriate and reasonable solution, there would be many contracts that I would have to break in order to do this, one of which was the original, "You need to be the caregiver in this family and then you will be loved in return."

I began to realize that I did not need to be everything to everyone. Once I identified and released the contract that it was okay to take care of myself first, I was able to release the fear that no one would love me. I needed to go still deeper within to discover my voice and to learn how to honor it. What I heard loudly and clearly was that I had become a toxic waste dump. I was poisoning myself with fearful and painful thoughts, feelings, memories, and contractual agreements, implicit and explicit. My sister-in-law called me a human version of Love Canal. Maybe, I suggested to a friend, I could get a government grant and get myself cleaned out!

Do you ignore your needs? Take a moment to stop and listen to your thoughts and feelings. What do you hear? What is it that you need to happen so that you can release your feelings of discomfort and dis-ease?

Receiving

Listening and receiving are sequential. Listening requires you to hear within rather than closing off, withdrawing, and retreating. If you are able to stay open, then you move to receiving. Receiving is the ability to welcome and accept your feelings and thoughts and to honor them. Receiving allows for a reconnection to your self, a move from conceptualizing to experiencing. Ultimately, you can reach a place of calm, with increased clarity and self-awareness. Receiving occurs when healing has taken place and self denial is replaced by self-acceptance and self-love.

I was being healed by the love that was being sent my way. I did not have to be brave and strong and assure myself and others that I was fine. I was not fine and I needed help. I wanted help. More importantly, I asked and allowed for this process to occur. I had turned a corner. I began to listen, trust, and receive my own voice and my own needs in a deeper, more profound way.

I was exploring all the places within that were strangling me. I began to question my internal messages about who I was supposed to be, what I was supposed to be doing, obligations I was supposed to meet, agreements I had made with myself and others and continued to try to fulfill. I had done pieces of this work over the years and thought I had released most of the limiting thoughts, feelings, fears, and behaviors. I had more work to do. I faced myself, dug in, and listened harder.

In my clinical work, I teach people how to release all the negative thoughts and feelings they can allow themselves to access and acknowledge. They must first give themselves permission to do the releasing, otherwise they will continue to hold onto their inner demons. I gave myself permission to face my own inner demons and to release them. This exploration led me to the understanding of the concept of contracts and how they control our lives from childhood through adulthood. I am clear that my path has changed and had I listened earlier on, I may not have had to go through a traumatic illness. I am, however, listening and receiving now with every fiber of my being. I chose to move on to the next part of my life.

It's time for you to move on to the next part of your life as well. It's time for you to release all the negative contracts that you've continued to cling onto and drag along with you. These contracts are holding you back and are limiting who you can be evolving into. It's time to rewrite these contracts and receive all the wonderful gifts that life has to offer to you.

Tools and Skills

Throughout this book, you will be given a variety of tools and skills to use. You will be shown different ways of gathering information. Having information will help you to become aware of how you experience and relate to yourself and others. Then you can make informed decisions about what changes you might want to make in your life. Once you have gathered information, you will need to know what to do with it, how to use it so that it benefits you. The skills and tools you will be given will assist you in this process. As you use the tools and skills, you will see shifts beginning to take place. Here are some of the tools and skills you will be using.

Journaling

It will be important for you to have a special journal to write in. This journal is a way to mark your progress. It is for you and no one else. Use it as a place to record your most private inner thoughts. Begin to understand that you no longer need to keep secrets about yourself from yourself. Use the journal to do the exercises in the book. Try to do some freewriting in your journal several times a week without censoring thoughts and feelings.

Exploring Yourself

These sections will provide you with important clues and useful information about yourself as well as how other people in your life have affected you. You will gain information about how you think, feel, operate, and function. If I ask you to reflect on something, I am asking you to stop and think quietly and calmly.

Scaling

Scaling is an effective and objective way to interpret information. I will ask you to do rating on a scale of 1 to 10, 1 being the lowest, and 10 the highest. Here is an example.
Rate the following:

* How willing am I to make changes in my life?

If you gave yourself a 4, this would tell you that you are not very motivated to make changes. If you gave yourself a 9, this would tell you that you are very motivated to make changes.
I might then follow up with:

* What needs to happen in order for you to move you up on the scale?

Once you have identified what you think needs to happen in order to move you up on the scale, you can begin to develop a plan to implement what needs to occur next. You are going to be learning how to do things step-by-step, so don't scare yourself by believing that you have to do everything all at once.

Meditating

Meditating will teach you how to soothe and comfort yourself. Meditating is a tool for becoming clearer about what is actually going on inside cognitively and emotionally, and allows you to discover important insights about what changes need to be made in order to enrich your life. Meditating enables you to become an observer of your thoughts. In a meditative state, your awareness and perception of ideas, images, thoughts, and feelings are amplified. The result is a sense of connection to yourself. This feeling of connection is experienced as feelings of inner safety, inner trust, and serenity. By observing, you will more easily identify struggles.

Meditating allows you to slow down and requires that you be in the present. Think about how much time you spend in the past, ruminating, obsessing, and regretting. Or are you in the future, trying to escape the past and the present? Here and now is where you need to learn to live your life and to experience feelings of inner peace and joy.

Through meditation you can:

- See more clearly how you experience yourself and others.

- Learn to respond rather than react to your life.

- Recognize and understand how you resist change.

- Learn how to acknowledge and release painful life experiences you have held onto without having to re-experience pain every time you have a memory.

- Understand more clearly why and how you replicate unhealthy patterns.

- Discover from within that you have the ability and power to change these patterns.

Beginning a Meditation

If you begin to experience anxiety or tension as you do the work in this book, it is because you are stirring up uncomfortable feelings and memories that you have not been able to feel in control of. In order to manage the discomfort, try using this meditation technique to quiet and calm yourself.

Put on soft, relaxing music. Find a comfortable place to sit or lie. Close your eyes and take several deep breaths in. Release any thoughts, worries, or concerns you may have just for now. If your mind wanders, gently refocus on the music. Allow the muscles in your body to relax. Find yourself becoming more and more comfortable, more and more relaxed with each breath that you take in. Release tension with each outbreath. If your mind wanders, refocus on the music or on your breathing. Begin all meditations this way.

Learning, Gifts, and Reinforcement

At the end of each chapter, I will ask you to write a paragraph about what you have learned. This is a way for you to organize the information you have received and begin to integrate it.

I will also ask you to write about the gifts that you have received as a result of what you have learned. If you really look, you will find that there are gifts that accompany all of life's experiences. I believe that every struggle we are faced with is there to teach us something we need to know about ourselves.

Using my experience of becoming ill, here are the gifts that I received.

1. I determined that I would not become a victim to my illness.

2. Each new day had a new beginning with new hope attached to it.

3. I realized I was important to others in a very real way. Not because I was "doing" for them, but because I was a person they loved, cared for, and valued.

4. I asked for help and allowed myself to receive it.

5. As a result of my experience, I created this book.

6. I determined that the process of writing this book would be a joyful journey and it has been.

You will be given an exercise to reinforce your learning. Here is a reinforcement exercise for this chapter.

Start to meditate daily in order to begin to learn how to calm, comfort, and soothe yourself. It is a pleasant way to begin or end the day. You can do it for 5 minutes or 25 minutes. The more you practice, the easier it will be to relax and the more deeply you will be able to go.

Concepts to Remember

These are the main ideas that were presented in the chapter.

1. You can be the person *you* choose to be.

2. You can take back your power.

3. Wake-up calls are there to prompt you to change what no longer works for you.

4. It's healthy to take care of yourself first.

5. Listening to your needs nourishes you.

6. Receiving is the ability to welcome and accept your feelings and thoughts and to honor them.

7. There are gifts that accompany all life's experiences.

Chapter 2

Contracts

How You Formed Your Identity

When you were growing up what you wanted and needed most was to feel loved, valued, and accepted. What you never wanted to happen was to feel excluded, unloved, or abandoned. In *Anatomy of the Spirit,* (1997) Caroline Myss talks about the concept of the tribal culture. Within a tribe or family, you form your identity, your sense of belonging, your sense of self. Here you learn what you need to do in order to conform to the family will so that you can get your needs met. You yield to the tribal belief system in order to fit in and belong. Aligning with the family belief system can be powerful and enhancing, or it can undermine and deplete your sense of personal power. This depends on what the family messages are and what contracts you made in order to accommodate to your family's expectations.

Making Accommodations

You did what you needed to do in order to belong and to have your needs met by your family. You made all kinds of accommodations in order to be loved, valued, and accepted. When you did not feel loved, valued, and accepted, you became confused, insecure, and depressed.

As a child, you experienced how your family operated, learned what the needs and expectations were, what your role was, and took your place within the family system. In doing so, you unwittingly made and played out internal contracts about who you would be in order to get what you needed.

Fulfilling Your Parents' Dreams

Your contracts either enhanced you or are still haunting you. If they are haunting you, it is because they are not giving you what you need. They are holding you back. The person you want to be is in conflict with the person your parents needed you to be, and you are still trying to be the good child. For example, if your parents needed you to fulfill their lost opportunities and dreams, you may have tried to accommodate them. But, if their needs and wishes conflicted with your needs and wishes, you ended up feeling frustrated and unhappy.

Alan wanted to be an artist. His father saw no value in this as a career and told him he would only pay for his college education if he studied engineering. Alan let go of his dream. When he had a son, he encouraged his creativity. His son was bright and talented and wanted to please his father. He became a graphic designer, although he really wanted to go to law school. He never really enjoyed his work, but he kept at it. He didn't want to disappoint his father and he didn't want his father to be disappointed in him.

Fulfilling a parent's dream can turn into a nightmare of resentment and disappointment. You do it for approval and acceptance but at a cost to yourself.

Exploring Yourself

* What did you have to do in order to fit into and accommodate to your family?

* What were your parents' dreams about what their lives would be?

* Did they achieve their dreams?

* Do you think this affected the messages they gave to you? In what way?

Your Need for Approval

Everything you did as a child revolved around your gaining your parents' approval. This was what motivated you to enter into your contracts. As an adult, are you still looking for approval? Take a moment and reflect on your need for approval from others now. Do you:

* Do things to please others so that you can get their approval?

* Do anything to avoid conflict?

* Go along with what someone else wants rather than expressing what you want?

* Take on blame when something goes wrong?

* Get confused about what your needs really are?

If you gained approval from your parents by accommodating to their needs and wishes, you are probably still trying to get that approval in all your relationships. You find yourself yearning for approval and will do almost anything to get it.

Your Family's Messages

Your family gave you messages about who you were expected to be. You may not have been seen for who you really were. Referring to the above example, you may have been seen as the person your parents *needed* you to be.

The family message may have been to get good grades. If you did well in school, your parents could bask in the limelight and you would receive the validation you needed and wanted from them. Another message might have been, "Don't question our authority." You learned to obey and to avoid conflict. Then maybe you would get the love and approval you sought.

If parenting styles were different in your family, you may have had one parent who gave you clear and consistent messages, while the other parent's messages were fuzzy and inconsistent. This created confusion and dissonance for you. You ended up feeling very conflicted and confused about who you were, who you were supposed to be, and what you were supposed to be doing.

The messages you received as a child were the foundation blocks that taught you who and how to be. You have carried your childhood messages into adulthood. How you think and feel about yourself and how you relate to others reflect the true power these messages held for you.

Mixed Signals

The messages given and the rules you followed in order to fit in and adapt to your family formed and shaped you. Sometimes the messages and rules were clear but sometimes you had to guess at what you thought they might be. Sometimes they made sense, sometimes they confused you. If you were told, "Don't cry because it upsets your mother," then you became aware that crying was a negative emotional response and it upset someone. Most likely, this message was not meant to be harmful. It was, however, a way to control the emotional energy of the family. "No one should be upset in this family. The expression of emotions causes bad things to happen." Small verbal messages can carry a significant amount of weight over a lifetime.

What then were you to do when you were upset, angry, hurting, sad, or fearful? If you expressed your feelings, you were being hurtful to the family and if you held your feelings in, you were being hurtful to yourself. Whatever decision you made was wrong.

Mixed signals about what you are feeling and what is acceptable to express create inner struggle and conflict. They leave you feeling confused about what is right and what is wrong, what is okay and what is not okay. You are always questioning what is normal to think and feel or how to behave. You don't know what is realistic or acceptable.

When you discover your childhood messages, you can then decide which ones have been helpful and which ones have been undermining for you. Then you can learn how to let go of the negative messages and create positive ones that allow you to feel good about yourself and lead to developing healthier relationships with others.

Exploring Yourself

What messages did you receive?

* Were you given the message that you were loved for who you were?

* How did your parents show their love?

* Were you given the message that you were valued and accepted? How did your parents let you know you were valued and accepted?

* Were you given messages of approval? How did your parents show approval?

* Were you allowed to freely express your feelings (anger, sadness, frustration, joy, love, disagreement)? If not, what did you do with these feelings?

* Were messages consistent?

While your parents gave you powerful messages about yourself, there were other people in your life that affected you as well. Siblings, grandparents, aunts and uncles, teachers, religious figures, even parents of friends may have influenced the way you thought and felt about yourself.

Exploring Yourself

List all the people that were powerful to you during your childhood. Next to their name, write the messages you received from them.

Safe Environments

One of the most important functions the family performs is to provide an emotionally safe, structured environment for everyone. When rules are clear, consistent, and reasonable, everyone knows what to expect. There is a sense of comfort and clarity that is internalized. When rules are sometimes followed and sometimes not, the environment feels confusing and chaotic and that is what is internalized.

Elizabeth grew up in a family that was loving and nurturing. Most of the messages she received were clear and consistent. When they weren't, she spoke up. One afternoon Elizabeth asked her mother if she could go to her friend's house to play. Without thinking things through, her mom said, "No." Elizabeth was upset, naturally. After a few minutes, mom realized how arbitrary she had been and went upstairs to apologize. She told Elizabeth that she was sorry and had decided it would be okay for her to visit her friend. Elizabeth became very angry. "I don't like it when you change your mind," she said. "It confuses me. I need you to say one thing and stick to it. If you need to think about it for awhile, just tell me you will let me know. If I don't like what you decide and am angry with you, then I'll just get over it."

Elizabeth explained to her mother, very graphically, what it felt like inside of her when she was not consistent. She demanded that her mother provide an emotionally safe environment for her. Because Elizabeth's parents listened to and valued her feelings, she was able to access and express them comfortably.

About Expectations

The expectations that were passed on to you about who and how to be shaped and molded you into the adult you are today. They taught you what was acceptable, or what was unacceptable in your family. Sometimes you may not have known what was acceptable and unacceptable because the rules and expectations changed constantly. What was okay yesterday isn't okay today.

Exploring Yourself

Let's begin by recognizing your family's rules and expectations.

As a child, did you:

* Clearly understand what was expected from you?

- Spend a great deal of time trying to guess who you were supposed to be? What you were supposed to be doing?

- Feel stupid because you thought you should know?

- Feel confused about what was okay and what was not?

- Feel frustrated a lot of the time?

As an adult, are you still struggling with:

- Knowing what is expected from you?

- Trying to figure out who you are supposed to be and what you are supposed to be doing?

- Feeling ashamed because you don't know what you think you ought to know?

- Feeling confused about what is okay and normal?

- Frustration around what is acceptable?

If you were given clear rules and expectations, you probably grew up in a family where making mistakes was part of the learning process and personal growth was encouraged. As a result, you are confident and are open to taking in new information.

If your family messages were mixed, you probably spent your childhood very carefully following any clue that was given to you about who you were supposed to be or what you were supposed to be doing. This left you confused about what to think and feel. You found it difficult to speak up and ask for clarification from anyone. You were always afraid of doing or saying the wrong thing and fearful that you would be found out and exposed. Your thoughts were, "I should know this, I must be stupid, there is something wrong with me, everyone else knows this." You were left guessing about what you should be thinking and what you should be feeling.

As an adult, you are still operating the way you did as a child. You are still looking for clues and you are still guessing, trying to figure out the correct answers. You are very cautious and careful and believe that you have to walk on eggshells. You still feel ashamed that you don't know the answers. Here's a secret I'll share with you. No one knows all the answers and everyone struggles in life. Some people just got healthier childhood messages than others. You don't, however, need to continue to go along with messages that are harmful to you. You will be learning how to change the messages and the contracts that go along with them.

Exploring Yourself

* What were the healthy messages that you received?

* What were the unhealthy messages that you received?

* What feelings come up for you when you think about growing up in your family?

These are feelings that you are still carrying within you and which you are still connected to. You may think that they have been left behind but they are with you every day. They are still influencing you and your relationships with others. They cause powerful reactions for you when they are triggered.

Your Childhood Contracts

Contracts can begin at birth. How is it that an infant intuitively understands what his or her role must be within a particular set of circumstances within a family? I am thinking of a young family with three children. The father was diagnosed with cancer and required a long course of chemotherapy and radiation. Shortly after his diagnosis, his wife discovered she was pregnant. This pregnancy was the hope for the future for these parents. The birth of a little boy provided a great source of pleasure and comfort to everyone. Because of the family turmoil around the father's illness, it seemed miraculous to them that this was such a good, quiet, and happy baby. Was this a coincidence, or was this child getting the message that he was expected to provide pleasure and comfort? He cried very little, slept well, and was very easy. "It's a good thing that Ben is such a good baby," said his grandmother. "I don't know what my daughter-in-law would have done if he'd been a difficult child. She has so much to contend with. He is so beautiful and makes everyone so happy."

The expectation for Ben was that he be good, quiet, and make others happy. He is easing the family pain. What does this portend for his future? Who will he think he is supposed to be, how many others will he believe he must please and take care of in his life, what if he fails?

At five months of age, Ben may have entered into a non-negotiated, very binding contract to be good and to be a source of comfort to those around him. If he does this, he will receive love and approval. I am not trying to say that Ben's parents intentionally set him up for struggle. They had no awareness he was internalizing their expectations and might be making a contract. What they are living with at the moment is great uncertainly, fear, pain, and potential loss of a beloved husband and father. This child is giving them tremendous pleasure. His life choices and relationships will, however, be greatly impacted as a result of the timing of his birth, what's going on in the family, and the messages he receives as a result. There is no blame to assign here. It is a matter of life's circumstances.

You were taught how to be by example and/or expectation. Whatever your family needed from you, you tried to provide so that you could receive what you needed from them. You made internal contracts and tried very hard to meet the terms of these contracts. In your adult relationships, you are probably doing the very same thing.

Your Parents' Contracts

It is important to note that your parents were bound to their own contracts. These contracts affected the messages they gave to you. Most parents love their children and want the best for them. When your parents made mistakes over and over again with you, it was not because that was their intent. Rather, it was because they didn't have the information, tools, and skills to do things differently.

If you are a parent, you can do things differently because you are becoming informed. You can learn to parent in a way that is healthy so that your children create healthy internal contracts. When your children are doing well and have good self-esteem as a result of what you are giving to them, you are, in a sense, reparenting your own self. Parenting well is an opportunity to heal your childhood wounds. You know what it felt like to get crazy, inconsistent messages. You know what it felt like to feel that you just weren't good enough. When you make a conscious decision to break and rewrite unhealthy contracts that affect your parenting style, you give your children a healthy, well-integrated childhood experience. When they feel good, you feel good.

The Operating Principle

The messages you received as a child evolved into internal contracts. These contracts were not mutual agreements between you and your parents, though you assumed this to be the case. You yearned for your dearest wish to be fulfilled, the wish to be loved and valued.

Contracts become powerful mind-sets and operating principles by which you think, act, feel, and behave. They serve to accommodate the family's needs and in return you hope you will get what you need. Contracts are based on necessity, expectation, and survival. They can be both positive and negative depending on whether the messages are healthy or unhealthy ones. They bind you to a lifelong set of thoughts, feelings, and behaviors. As adults, you continue to play out your childhood contracts even when they are not working for you. You do so because you are unaware that you have made contracts. Even when you figure this out, you don't know how to break them or how to rewrite them. You just keep trying to apply your contracts to all your relationships, trying to get what you need by being who you think you need to be.

Children will do anything in order to earn love and acceptance. When you repeatedly tried and didn't receive what you needed emotionally, you came to believe there was something wrong with you. You assumed *you* were deficient in some way when you experienced hurt or rejection. You believed this because you didn't have the intellectual or developmental awareness that it is the parent, or some other powerful person in your life, that may be limited or destructive to you physically, emotionally, or spiritually. While you were turning yourself inside out in order to prove you were worthy, it wasn't working and you were being given a message that it was because you were not deserving. You internalized this message and believed you were not good enough and were unlovable. You still believe this.

Healthy Contracts

If your family messages were healthy, the contracts you made were enhancing and growth producing. These are examples of healthy messages, childhood contracts, and how they play out in adulthood.

Message: We will always love you because you are you.

Childhood Contract: I don't have to try to make you love me. I am accepted and valued as I am.

Adulthood: I am loveable. I don't have to keep proving myself to others in order to get them to love me.

* * * * *

Message: Your feelings are important to us and we will listen to them and be respectful of them.

Childhood Contract: I can tell you how and what I feel. What I feel is important to you and you will respect my feelings.

Adult: Who I am and what I feel are important. It is okay for me to express my feelings and to ask for what I want and need from others.

* * * * *

Message: You are the child in this family and you will be taken care of.

Childhood Contract: I can be a child and I can depend on my parents to take care of me.

Adult: I don't have to be the caregiver in relationships in order to feel good about myself or to get love. My relationships can be mutually interdependent.

* * * * *

Message: We will tell you what our expectations are and
we will follow through with what we say.

Childhood   When I need information about what is expected
Contract: from me, I can trust that my parents will tell me
and will mean what they say.

Adult: I don't have to guess at what people mean.
I know what is reasonable and if I get confused
in an interaction, I can ask for clarification.

* * * * *

Message: We will treat you with love and respect.

Childhood   I can make mistakes and still receive my parents'
Contract: love.

Adult: People treat one another reasonably and with
respect. If they don't, I don't have to be in a
relationship with them.

* * * * *

Message: We believe in you.

Childhood   I can feel good about following my instincts.
Contract: I can try new things and ask for help when
I need to.

Adult: I am able to take risks. I can function
independently. I am a resourceful person.

* * * * *

Healthy messages showed you that you were loved, valued,
and respected. They were grounding and stabilizing and taught
you in positive ways about trust and intimacy. They provided an
environment of emotional, psychological, and physical well-being,
and safety within the family. They were uncomplicated. They presented you with affirming, growth-filled, foundational messages
that led to the creation of healthy internal contracts. Children
from emotionally healthy families are comfortable with their
thoughts and feelings, can access and express these thoughts and

feelings, and move into adulthood unconflicted, confident, and emotionally in tune, at least a good part of the time.

It is important to state that there is no such thing as the "perfect" family or the "perfect" childhood. Most people get a mixture of both positive and negative messages. Parents do some things very well and other things not quite so well. In a basically loving, caring, nurturing family, healthy messages are reinforced by the constancy of the parents' comforting responses and actions. You learned to trust that your parents would provide for your needs. They taught you how to comfort and soothe yourself when there was internal or external upset.

Unhealthy Contracts

If your childhood messages were repeatedly unhealthy, they reinforced your negative self-concept. Contracts based on these messages were undermining to your sense of self and your ability to trust in the world. These are examples of unhealthy messages, childhood contracts, and how they play out in adulthood.

Message: We don't talk about feelings in this family.

Childhood Contract: I have to hide my feelings, otherwise my parents will be angry with me. If I do this, my parents will love me.

Adult: I can't express my feelings. If I do, people will disapprove of me and they won't like me.

                    * * * * *

Message: Be good, do as you are told, don't create any conflict.

Childhood Contract: I will be good, I will do whatever you tell me to do, and you will love me.

Adult: Being good means pleasing others. It means that I will do everything I can in order to avoid conflict. I will make sure that everyone is happy. Then everyone will like me.

                    * * * * *

Message: I am not interested in your opinions.

Childhood   I will not express my thoughts because they are not
Contract: important to you. You will like me if I do this.

Adult: I have no right to express myself. What I think is
              not important or valuable or of interest to
              anyone anyway.

* * * * *

Message: You can't do anything right.

Childhood   I will try very hard to do what you need for me
Contract: to do and then you will accept me.

Adult: Nothing I do will ever be good enough no matter
              how hard I try. I will always fail. I have no power.

* * * * *

Message: It's your fault my life is unhappy.

Childhood   I will try to make you happy and we will be a
Contract: happy family.

Adult: It's my responsibility to make people happy.

* * * * *

Message: You make me angry and that's why I have to
              hurt you.

Childhood   I won't make you angry, I will be good, and
Contract: then I will be safe.

Adult: I will never feel safe or trust anyone and it is my
              fault. I am bad.

* * * * *

Unhealthy messages created feelings of confusion and fear. They were destabilizing and inhibited your ability to develop healthy, intimate, trusting relationships. The contracts that came out of these messages bound you to feelings of pain and disappointment in yourself and others. They affected your ability to trust your feelings and thoughts. They undermined your self-esteem. They hurt you deeply. They wounded and damaged your spirit. You moved into adulthood conflicted, insecure, and emotionally out of balance. You are uncomfortable and insecure within yourself and in your relationships with others because you are unable to access, trust, and express your true feelings and thoughts.

You created and agreed to contracts early in your life so that you could get the love, affirmation, and validation you needed from your parents and from anyone else who was important to you. You moved into adulthood conflicted, and are emotionally out of balance. You are still carrying within yourself these internalized contracts. You are continuing to make and abide by contracts that you hope will fulfill your needs. You are still trying to be the good child.

Your adult contracts are based on your childhood contracts. And they are still not giving you what you want and need. You continue to find yourself getting stuck in the same negative places and hitting the same unbending walls. This is because your contracts are built on a very shaky foundation. You try again and again to make the impossible work, because you are drawn to people and situations that bring up similar struggles and conflicts, and you keep applying the same techniques that didn't work in the first place. You are unaware that you have made contracts and of how binding these contracts are.

Some contracts are healthy and growth producing. Other contracts impair your belief in yourself. In order to change destructive feelings, thoughts, and behaviors, you must become aware of your patterns, themes, and internal messages so that you can identify what your contracts are. Only then can you give yourself the opportunity for change. Making change takes courage and a willingness to face inner demons. It is, however, the only way to release yourself from contracts that are limiting your ability to ascend to the joy that you have the right to experience in this life.

Being in Charge

Remember that you are in charge of your healing process. The goal is to gain insight into the powerful forces within that are either enhancing or undermining your life. Choosing to go on a new path requires commitment and effort. It will probably bring up some fears about what you might find within yourself. We all have places of shame, but holding onto the shame gives it more power than acknowledging and releasing it. We all have memories that we want to avoid; however, avoiding them gives them more power.

Making internal shifts is a process that takes time. It means letting go of what may feel comfortably uncomfortable. You know where you are now; maybe it's not great but you are familiar with it. If you let go, you may not know where you'll land. Change means taking a risk. Taking risks can be very scary. Making a commitment to developing a healthy self is something only you can choose.

The road will probably be bumpy at first. Facing inner demons can be scary and difficult, but you are being given tools to release these demons. Remember that holding onto emotional pain only serves to keep it in. Not thinking about or acknowledging the pain does not mean it isn't there. It just means that you are using a great deal of energy to block it from your conscious self. One way or another, however, the pain will seep out.

There is no right or wrong way to be doing this work. Move into it at a pace that is comfortable for you. No one is judging you. No one is looking over your shoulder. What is important is that you have made a decision to begin to identify and understand the hurt inside so that you can release it and create the life you want to be living. Sometimes it's hard to believe that things can change and be good when there's been so much bad. But you can get there, step-by-step, one day at a time; and in a way that works for you.

Believing You Can Do It

Begin to give yourself the message, "I can do this." I believe you can do it. You will take steps back at times, you will get caught up in old negative behaviors. The difference will be that as you learn about yourself, why you think or act in certain ways, you will be able to recognize what is going on and stop the negative process.

I had an obese client who was trying to diet. She did very well until she went to a party and lost control. When she came in to see me the next week, she said that she had failed her diet, felt terrible, and had given up. I looked at it another way. "Okay, you got offtrack, but you can start again right now. Next time you go to a party, plan ahead of time how you want to handle it. Learn from your experience, stop beating yourself up, know that you are human, forgive yourself, and continue on with your diet. This is just a setback, not the end."

So this is my message to you. Changing feelings, thoughts, and behaviors and evolving takes time. Meanwhile, be patient with yourself and accept that you are in a learning phase. When you slip, pick yourself up and try again. No one just does it right the first time. It takes practice. You'll get there in your own time. What is most important is not *when* it happens but *that* it happens.

Meditation

Start the meditation as described in chapter one. Visualize a beam of healing light flowing in through you. Feel the warmth of the light as it expands into each part of your body. Imagine this is love flowing through your entire being and allow yourself to feel immersed in it and comforted by it. Keep breathing in the light. Stay with this feeling as long as you wish and know you may bring yourself back to this place of peace and calm whenever you choose.

Learning, Gifts, and Reinforcement

Write a paragraph about what you have identified and learned from this chapter. What did you struggle with? What was comfortable for you? How are the struggles familiar for you?

What gifts can you take from what you have learned?

Practice the art of silence. In the morning, sit or lie down and be with yourself in the present and meditate from ten to twenty-five minutes. Take a walk, listen to the sounds around you, notice your surroundings, experience your breath. During the day, become aware of your body tension and give yourself permission to release the tension. Find a quiet place, breathe in slowly, and let go of thoughts and worries for five minutes. When driving, turn off the radio and be in the silence. When at home, turn off the television and be in the silence. Tell yourself that you are making a commitment to healing and being whole, and you deserve this.

Concepts to Remember

1. Your family taught you who to be and how to be.

2. Your family needed to provide an emotionally safe and structured environment in order for you to internalize healthy messages.

3. The messages you received as a child evolved into contracts. These contracts became powerful mind-sets and operating principles by which you thought, felt, and behaved. They accommodated the family's needs and in return you hoped to receive what you needed.

4. Contracts are based on necessity, expectation, and survival.

5. You continue to play out your contracts as an adult.

6. Healthy messages produce healthy contracts. Unhealthy messages produce unhealthy contracts.

7. You make contracts throughout your life based on your childhood contracts.

8. You are in charge.

9. Believe you can get there.

Chapter 3

The Power of Contracts

Entering into Contracts

When you entered into your childhood contracts, you committed to choices and decisions that would have an ongoing impact on your sense of yourself, and your relationships with others. The messages you received from your parents became internal demands. For example, "Be good," evolved into, "I *have* to be good." The need to reduce the anxiety that was generated by these internalized demands became a powerful driving force that guided and directed you. The contracts you made and bound yourself to were your way of managing these demands.

You believed your needs would be met if you fulfilled the terms of the internal contracts you made. However, these contracts that you entered into were unspoken and unacknowledged agreements that you struck with yourself. Sometimes you thought the contracts were with your parents, who knew nothing about them. "If I give my parents what they want and need," you thought, "they will give me what I want and need." Sometimes though, your contracts weren't about pleasing your parents. They were a coping mechanism. These contracts were the way in which you tried to protect yourself from being hurt by life's assaults.

The Power of Contracts

When you were a child, your contracts were powerful to you because you believed in them so deeply (even when your conscious self was unaware that you had made them). You believed:

* Your commitment to them would provide you with what you needed.

* They would protect you and would change the uncomfortable dynamic of your relationship to your parents.

* You would find the acceptance, belonging, and safety you longed for.

As an adult, you are still operating under the principle that if you honor your contracts, you will get what you need. You are still bound to them and you still believe in them.

The World of Contracts

Contracts are powerful and very binding. There are many types of contracts that you may enter into and you might agree to more than one simultaneously. Let's explore several contracts so that you can get a clearer picture of how different family situations might have led you into some of your contracts.

I Won't Be a Burden

If your parents were struggling in any way, you may have been given a message to not rock the family boat. What you understood was, "We have too much to handle, don't burden us with anything else." This happened to Amy.

Amy has a history of eating disorders and low self-esteem. She says she has "hit a wall." "I think I know what I want but I just can't seem to get there, and I don't know what is stopping me."

When Amy was two, her mother became very ill. Her father was left to care for Amy, her baby sister, and his sick wife. Amy helped with her younger sister and never asked her mom or dad for anything. She learned to keep her feelings in because no one had the time or energy for her. In her senior year of high school, she applied to art school and did not ask for help with the application process, which required her to photograph all her artwork. She did this all on her own.

Amy was twenty-three when she married Alan. She says she chose him because he paid attention to her and this made her feel valued. After eleven years of marriage, she is surprised that she is now his emotional caregiver. She is unable to ask Alan for even the smallest bit of help either emotionally or with their five-year-old daughter. She feels that she allows Alan to control her. She struggles with trusting her instincts, abilities, and feelings and is unable to speak up.

Amy's childhood message was to not be a burden to her parents and to do as she was told. Her contract was, "I will be self-reliant and not ask for anything, then Mom and Dad will love me." As an adult, Amy believes she has to do what others expect of her. She still cannot ask for help. "What I feel and who I am are not important," she says. "I have no voice."

You Won't Control Me

If your emotional needs were continually unmet, you may have given up the hope that things could change. You may have become outwardly angry and rebellious, as a way to demand the attention you desired, or you may have thought, "The hell with you." Rebellion may be the only way you had any power in your relationship with your parents.

The original contract, "I will be who you need me to be, do what you need me to do," failed because you did not get what you needed or wanted in return. You may have terminated the existing contract and replaced it with another contract that said, "I refuse to be who you need or want me to be or do." As long as you were going to be disappointed, you might as well be the one to control the situation. This is a child who gave up the hope that his needs would be met.

Dan describes himself as having been "a bad kid." "My father never told me he loved me. He only told me what I did wrong. He was very rigid and controlling. I decided that he was not going to run my life," he said. "I got into drugs, I ran away. I

did anything I could to show him that he had no power over me."
Yet inside, Dan felt powerless and depressed. He has been married and divorced twice.

Dan's message was that he was a bad child. His contract
was, "I will do what I want to do and you won't be able to control
me." As an adult, Dan believes that he can't let himself trust or
open up to anyone. "If I do, they'll control me."

I Will Take Care of You

Sometimes a parent relies on their children to take care of
them. If this happened to you, you may not feel you have the
right to enjoy your own life when your parents are depending on
you to take care of them either physically, emotionally, or spiritually. This happened to Diana.

Diana is thirty-eight, single, and lives at home. She has an
older, married sister who lives in another state. Diana says that
growing up in her family was painful because her parents' marriage was filled with anger and tension, and she was always in the
middle, trying to mediate the anger between them. She has had a
strong connection to her mother, who is depressed, and feels she
needs to be there for her. She experienced her father as being
critical and neither a loving parent nor loving husband. She
wanted very much to have a connection to him but could never
find a way in. Her relationships with men have been unsuccessful
because the men she attracts are emotionally unavailable.

There are two major contracts that Diana is bound to. One
has to do with her mother, who gave her the message, "I need
you to take care of me." Her contract with her mother is, "It is my
responsibility to take care of you and provide for your comfort. I
want you to be okay." As a result of this contract, she believes she
can't live a life for herself.

Her second contract is around her father. Her message from
him was, "I am emotionally unavailable to you." Her contract
became, "I will try to make a connection with you so you will love
me." But that never happened for Diana. As a result, she believes
men cannot be trusted and she plays this out by choosing men
who are unwilling or unable to make an emotional commitment
to her.

I Won't Get Attached

Abandonment or the death of a parent might have left you with deep wounds. There are feelings of betrayal, sadness, anger, fear, and an eternal longing for that parent to return to provide the love that has been so cruelly lost. To manage and cope with this loss, you might have made a contract to shut down emotionally in order to protect yourself from the pain that has been generated. This is Les's story.

Les was five when his father died suddenly. His family was devastated. His whole life changed in a moment. Les's mother was forced to go out to work and he was left in the care of an older sibling. "I hated what was happening. I was so angry with my father for dying and leaving me. And I was also angry with my mother for leaving me. Even though I knew she had to work to support us, I didn't care. I was just hurting all the time. I remember thinking that I would never get married when I grew up because what if something happened? I never wanted to get attached to anyone ever again." At forty, Les is still single but is questioning if this is what he really wants.

Les's message was that people kept leaving. His contract was, "I won't let myself get attached, then I won't be hurt." As an adult, he still believes it is not safe to become attached to anyone because he is afraid he will be left.

I Won't Live Your Life

Making life decisions that are based on not repeating or replicating your parents' lives can get you sidetracked. You are determined to do it differently because you saw and experienced your parents' unhappiness or because they expected or demanded that you do it better than they did. You may end up lost on a path that you never really wanted to be on. Dierdre got caught up in this dilemma.

Dierdre was the third in a family of six girls. Her mother had married young. Her father was demanding and controlling and was away on business much of the time. This left Dierdre's mother home with all the responsibility for taking care of a large family and a large house. Her mother was always stressed and unhappy.

At forty, Dierdre is an unmarried single mother. She is struggling with whether or not to marry a man she loves. She very much wants a second child but is afraid if she gets married, she will lose herself and will no longer be able to be independent. She acknowledges that much of her drive to be independent and successful has to do with not being her mother.

The message Dierdre received from her mother was: "Being married ruins your life." So, she made a contract: "I will have a career and will be fiercely independent. I won't live my mother's life." As an adult, Dierdre believes that she can only be independent if she is on her own. She wonders if her life choices are more about not living her mother's life than about living a life she wants.

I Deserve to Suffer

Religious messages that intertwine with family messages may have had a powerful influence on your development. These messages are instrumental in the formation of lifelong thoughts, feelings, and actions. This was true for Beverly.

Beverly was brought up as a Catholic and was taught by the nuns within her church school that you must suffer in order to be a spiritual (i.e. worthy) person. "Jesus had to suffer and die for something he didn't do. This message was reinforced in my family. There was no laughter, no joy, and no freedom to express thoughts or feelings. My parents were tense all the time, everything was always a lot of work that never ended," she told me. "All the messages I received as a child reinforced my belief that I was bad and nothing I did would ever be good enough in my parents' eyes, or in God's eyes."

Beverly believed she was so sinful that before she married her husband, she felt she had to confess to him all the bad things she had thought or done in her life. If he still wanted to marry her, then she would know he loved her. She and her husband raised three severely abused, adopted children. There were many difficulties that strained her marital relationship. "I've done the best I could do to give everyone love and understanding, but I don't think it was good enough. I don't think I've been good enough."

Beverly's message was, "Suffering is necessary in order to be a deserving person." She made a contract that stated that she needed to be responsible for the well-being of others and that she must endure pain, and only then she could earn love. As an adult, Beverly believes she must give all of herself to others, and she hopes then they will love her. But, she also believes that this will never happen, because she will never be good enough or deserving enough to be loved.

All these contracts were made in response to family needs and expectations. When you formulated your initial childhood contracts, you did so hoping that if you agreed to their terms and fulfilled them, you would be rewarded with what you needed, wanted, and desired—unconditional and unreserved love, acceptance, nurturing, support, attention, and survival. When you did not receive what you hoped for, you became disappointed, disenchanted, and disillusioned. As an adult, you are still bound to your childhood contracts and are still not reaping the rewards from them.

Exploring Yourself

Now that the concept of contracts is clearer to you, see if you can name your childhood messages and contracts. As you do more work in this book, you will discover additional contracts.

Childhood Message   **Contract**

1.   1.

2.   2.

3.   3.

* * * * *

Complementary and Conflicting Contracts

Some contracts piggyback onto others, and are complementary. For example, if your parents were supportive, nurturing, and accepting, you may have made a contract that stated, "I will do well in anything I set my mind to do," and another that stated, "It's okay for me to express my thoughts." These two contracts fit together. You can be successful because you feel good about who you are and you feel comfortable expressing yourself. These would be complementary contracts.

But, let's say you had an alcoholic mother. When she was drinking, she went into rages and would then apologize to you and promise she wouldn't drink anymore. You wanted very much to believe her. She needed you to believe her. So, you made a contract that said, "I will believe that you won't drink anymore." She never followed through. So you made another contract, "I can't trust you." You made this second contract in order to protect yourself from being hurt and disappointed. These are two difficult and conflicting contracts. You're trying to believe someone you don't trust. This set of contracts is crazy making.

Exploring Yourself

* Do you see any complementary contracts on your list?

* Do you see any conflicting contracts on your list?

* Which childhood contracts evolved into adult contracts?

* How have these contracts affected the life choices you have made? For example, would you have chosen a

different career, a different partner, different friends? Would you be more adventurous, less fearful? Would you relate to people differently?

When you know what your contracts are, you can begin to see how they have influenced the choices you have made in your life to this point. Your childhood contracts were and are powerful to you because your foundational beliefs about who you were and what you could expect from your parents and from your life became set and fixed. Every experience and every relationship you have entered into has been colored by these initial contracts.

Exploring Yourself

Refer to your contracts:

* Which contracts are enhancing to you?

* Which contracts are undermining to you?

* What are your most powerful contracts?

* What makes these contracts so powerful for you?

* What feelings do you experience when you think about the effect these contracts have had on your life?

Meditation

This is an exercise that teaches you how to calm and soothe yourself. Take a moment and think about a place that would provide comfort and safety for you. A place that feels peaceful and nurturing. It can be a place you have visited, a room in your home, a memory of something that was pleasant, a place you have dreamed about going to, or a fantasy. When you have discovered this ideal place for yourself, close your eyes and visualize your safe place. Remain in this safe place for as long as you wish. The more you practice this exercise, the more easily you will relax into it. You can use this image when you feel stressed or anxious and need a respite.

Learning, Gifts, and Reinforcement

What do you now understand about the contracts you made in childhood and their impact on your life? Who are you angry with or pleased with as a result? What regrets do you have?

What gifts have you received as a result of having discovered your childhood contracts?

Practice being in your safe place. Begin and end your day with this visualization.

Concepts to Remember

1. When you entered into your childhood contracts, you committed to choices and decisions that have had an ongoing impact on your life.

2. Your contracts are powerful because you believe they will bring you what you need.

3. Trusting your thoughts and feelings connects you to your intuitive self.

4. Every experience and every relationship we encounter is filtered through our childhood contracts.

Chapter 4

The Legacy of Contracts

Legacies

With loving, reinforcing messages, you entered into healthy, empowering contracts. You integrated a positive belief system, and were able to dream and envision a future filled with options and possibilities. You felt loved, valued, and accepted. You had confidence in yourself and learned that you could trust in others.

With confusing or negative messages, you integrated a belief system that constantly undermined you. You entered into unhealthy, disempowering contracts. You had difficulty envisioning a future that felt promising. If you did have dreams about your future, you may have had difficulty believing they were really within your reach. You believed you were unlovable, inadequate, and questioned whether you could trust others. As a result, you experienced feelings of:

* Shame

* Fear

* Sadness

* Doubt

* Rejection

You had to find a way to manage these uncomfortable thoughts and feelings. Maybe you pulled inward. Maybe you rebelled. Maybe you just shut down altogether.

As you moved into adulthood, you carried with you all these positive or negative thoughts and emotions. They became your legacy, your inheritance. As a result of your childhood messages and the subsequent contracts you have made, you are carrying a large suitcase filled with many legacies. Some are useful, others are hurting you. Though your body has grown, you have brought along with you the emotional experiences of the little boy or girl you once were.

If your suitcase is too a heavy burden, it is because the legacies you are carrying inside are hampering your ability to live your life fully. These legacies are undermining your feelings about yourself and they are impeding your potential to develop and maintain good, solid, loving relationships.

Pretending to Be Okay

Here is one legacy you may be carrying in your suitcase. When you were unable to get your needs met, you might have made a contract to ignore and bury your needs. You got the message that your needs were unacceptable. You translated this into, "I am unacceptable." To cope, you developed another contract. "I will pretend to be okay." You presented a self to the outside world that gave the impression that you were just fine. You presented a smiling face, a friendly demeanor, the picture of a happy child. Inside, however, there were feelings of shame, guilt, sadness, or anger that you had to push down. These were your real feelings but you were unable or not allowed to express them. Maybe you became numb. You had to do something with all these painful, hurtful thoughts, feelings, and experiences.

Exploring Yourself

* What feelings did you push down as a child?

* What feelings do you push down now?

* Are you still pretending that you are okay?

Living in the Shadow of Your True Self

When you pushed your feelings inward and started pretending, you began living in the shadow of your true self. This is where all the hurtful memories and experiences reside and where inner demons have taken command. The inner demons represent fears, doubts, and pain. You made a childhood contract to live in the shadow of your true self, because you were too afraid to acknowledge your real feelings and to express them. You were afraid you would be:

* Rejected

* Abandoned

* Punished

* Made fun of

* Ignored

If you made a contract to pretend you were okay, you lived in the shadow of the self you were meant to be. You accommodated to the environment you grew up in and to the people who controlled that environment. You are still living in the shadows.

Exploring Yourself

* Describe your pretend self.

* If you had been allowed to express your thoughts and feelings, what would they have been?

* What are they now?

Being Fearful

If you grew up in an environment that was non-nurturing, or was dangerous in some way, you felt fearful and alone. You felt vulnerable and powerless. You may have made a contract to be very, very good so you could be safe. This was the only way you could think of to make the bad things stop. But the bad things did not stop. As an adult, you are still fearful, vulnerable and you feel very much alone, even when you are surrounded by others.

Exploring Yourself

* Make a list of the things you were afraid of as a child.

* Make a list of the things you are afraid of now.

* Compare the lists.

Needing to Protect Yourself

To get through your childhood, you may have needed to find ways to protect yourself. You might have made a contract to not let anyone hurt you again. Do you remember Les's story? He was the five-year-old whose father died and he decided not to get attached to anyone ever again. If you remain connected to feelings of loss, you continue to focus on what is painful for you. You may find that now, even when you try to be positive and hopeful, you somehow keep ending up in the same lonely, isolated places because, in order to protect yourself, you have built inner emotional walls. While you think these walls are keeping fearful things and people out, they are also keeping you locked away, isolated, and alone from what you want and yearn for most—love and connection.

When you stay behind your walls, you re-create what you want least—disconnection, isolation, and loneliness. You are unable to see your own complicity in replicating your past experiences. You are unaware of the childhood contracts you have entered into and how you keep struggling to make them work so that you won't be hurt once again. But you do keep being hurt.

Hypervigilance

Living with a parent who is frequently triggered trains a child to be hyperaware of moods, words, shifts in behavior, and physical cues. If you pay careful attention, maybe you can prevent the eruption you see coming. Maybe you can control the outcome. This is how Kara coped.

"When my father's mouth began to twitch, I knew he was beginning to get upset. So if I would say something funny, or try to divert him in some way, then he might not blow up." Kara made a contract to be the family entertainer. Her legacy is that at age fifty-nine, she still feels responsible for providing entertainment in order to deflect any tension she senses in a situation. The stress of this is taking a physical toll on her and she suffers from severe migraine headaches.

Are you hypervigilant? Are you always looking for the place where you need to step in to mediate any tension you see beginning to build?

Carrying Wounds

The theory of childhood contracts is based on the expectation that if you did what you thought your parents wanted or expected, you would get what you needed from them. So, you did your dances and sang your songs to the best of your ability. When you really believed your performance was stellar and still you didn't receive the applause you yearned for, you asked yourself, "What am I doing wrong?" You never asked this question out loud because you were sure you would hear that you were at fault. "If I try harder," you thought, "if I say this instead of that, if I listen better, if I . . ." Nothing made a difference. Sometimes you may have gotten what you needed. Other times you didn't. There may have been no rhyme or reason to it. All you knew was that you were hurting. You wanted to be listened to, accepted, loved, and to feel okay instead of feeling hurt over and over again.

If your individuality was not respected, if you were not given positive feedback, and if you didn't feel valued, you became wounded. Whatever contract you made to do things better didn't work. So maybe you made another contract, "If I do this instead of that, if I am just as good as I can be, I'll get what I need." But no matter how good you were, how hard you tried, you still did not get what you needed. Your wounds became deeper and deeper.

As an adult, your legacy is that you are very sensitive and easily wounded. You may find that you become very defensive as a way to protect yourself when you feel hurt. If someone gives you feedback that feels critical to you in any way, you may have a big reaction, as Lili did.

Lili spent several hours making a lasagna for dinner. She asked her husband, Peter, if he liked it. Peter said it was good, but maybe it could use a little crushed red pepper to spice it up. Lili exploded. "Whatever I do, whatever I cook, it's never good enough, is it? I'm never making lasagna again."

Peter was stunned. "All I said was maybe it could use some red pepper. It's good, Lili, really it is. I don't understand why you are so upset."

Lili's family messages were critical and demanding. Her contract was to do whatever she had to in order to get her parents' approval. But no matter how hard she worked at trying to please them, she never felt she earned their approval. Peter's comment about the lasagna needing a little pepper brought up all her old wounds and caused her to feel that she had failed yet again. She was resentful that she had spent so much time making the dinner and hurt that Peter hadn't said it was wonderful.

Obviously, Lili overreacted. But when you have been hurt over and over again in childhood, you develop wounds. These are wounds you take with you into your adulthood. All the hurtful experiences and painful memories come right along with you into your adult self.

Exploring Yourself

* What are your childhood wounds about?

* Can you identify what triggers them?

* How do you usually react when your wounds are triggered?

Connecting Love to Pain

If love was connected to pain, then this will be what you think love is about. You made contracts to be good so you could get love. Well, maybe you got some love, but how you got it confused you. For example, if you were sexually abused and told it was because you were so loved and so special, you were all mixed up about love because what was happening to you didn't feel right. If you were abandoned by a parent due to death or divorce or if your parents had other relationships and people kept coming and going in your life, you were always experiencing loss. You were continually connecting and then having to disconnect. Love was not very steady, stable, or reliable.

It may have been that your parents were not good at expressing loving feelings or thoughts to you. This didn't mean you weren't loved, but you were wounded anyway. When there was no constancy in how your parents expressed their love to you, or when they were unable to follow through with actions that conveyed their love, you never learned to trust that love was something you could rely on to be there for you.

As an adult, you still connect love with pain. In order to experience one, you believe you will have to experience the other. Therefore, letting someone in is very scary for you. Letting someone in is to risk being hurt, rejected, and in the end, abandoned.

Rejecting Love

You need and want to be loved, but you may have been so hurt in your past that your fears about love and pain are stronger than your ability to let it in. You may make a contract to reject love so you won't be rejected first. You may sabotage your relationships without meaning or wanting to, but you can't allow yourself to be hurt anymore. You reach for love, then reject it because you are afraid. Then you experience pain. You are fulfilling your own fears. And each time you are hurt, you close off a little more of yourself. You run the risk of losing the ability to feel anything. You run the risk of spending your life robotically maneuvering through each day and expending your energies in deflecting anything that could potentially hurt you. Because you feel powerless, you try to control everything and everyone in your environment, which results in your pushing love away.

Exploring Yourself

* How is love connected to pain for you?

* Have you ever rejected love? When?

Giving Yourself Away

You may, on the other hand, give yourself away to others in your relationships. "If I love you enough, you'll love me back," reads this contract. You may reveal too much too soon and thrust yourself too quickly into relationships, hoping that this next partner will take care of your vulnerable self. You are needy and dependent, and make others responsible for who you are and what you feel. You have unrealistic fantasies and expectations about perfect love. You idealize and empower your new partners, endowing them with almost angelic or godlike qualities that no real human being could realistically possess.

When you begin to see this once flawless other as the real person they are, that they make mistakes, they say and do the wrong things, that they are imperfect, you become disappointed, angry, and feel a tremendous sense of betrayal and loss. You don't understand why your partners fail to provide what you want and need. The truth is that no one could ever really satisfy your needs, because they come from so deeply within you that nothing could fill you up.

So, it is reconfirmed that you can't trust love. It is reconfirmed that you are unlovable. Your childhood wounds have become your adult wounds and never seem to heal. Because you stick to the scripts of your childhood contracts, "If I do this, or say that, I will get what I need," you keep replaying the same scenes and outcomes.

Exploring Yourself

1. What are the messages you give to yourself about what love is?

2. What do you expect from your love relationships?

3. Are these expectations realistic?

4. Who have you loved?

5. Who has loved you?

Manipulating Love

You may use all kinds of methods to manipulate your partners into doing what you want and need them to do, which is to love you. This contract reads, "I will do what I have to in order to get you to love me." You might be soft and seductive in one moment, then become threatening and enraged in the next moment when you can't get what you want. Power and control become the name of your game. Being manipulative doesn't really feel very good to you, but because you never get what you really want—unconditional acceptance and love—you don't know what else to do.

What you discover is that the more you try to control things, the more they spin out of control. Until you believe you really deserve love, you will put yourself and anyone you are in a relationship with through challenges, tests, and roller-coaster rides.

Exploring Yourself

* Can you think of times when you were manipulative in your love relationships so that you could get what you needed?

* What did you do?

* How did that feel?

Believing You Are Unlovable

In order to allow someone in to love you, you must be able to accept that you are lovable. If the terms of your contracts were breached, if you weren't given consistently loving, nurturing messages, you didn't internalize the experience of feeling loved. When you don't internalize loving feelings, you believe you are unlovable. Why would you believe anyone else could love you? The experience of being loved may have no meaning for you. You may not know what love is, let alone how to love yourself or how to let others in to love you.

The feeling of self-love is one of self-acceptance, being able to internally say, feel, and believe statements such as, "I'm all right, I feel deserving, I feel valuable, I feel that I am worthy, I feel lovable." When you feel there is something wrong with you, how are you going to allow anyone in to love you? How could anyone love you? You do not feel deserving of being loved. You feel that you are defective. These may be the messages that you received.

If your childhood messages were positive about who you were, not about who you were expected to be or what you were expected to do, but honest and total acceptance and approval, then the experience of being loved feels comfortable. If you did not experience acceptance in this way, then being unconditionally loved is foreign to you and you will continue to yearn for the perfect love that you never received in the first place. You will go from relationship to relationship hoping that in this next connection your childhood contracts will be acknowledged and you will finally reap the rewards from all the effort you have exerted.

What is so painful is that you have entered into binding agreements that are binding only to you. They have not been mutually agreed upon. You are the only one who knows about them, yet you are not aware that this is so. You assume that there is an understanding that if you do what you believe is expected of you, you will be responded to in kind. You make the same assumption in your adult relationships. And you continue to be disappointed.

Believing You Have Failed

When love and acceptance failed to materialize, when your childhood contracts failed, you began to feel that you failed to fulfill your part of the agreement. You carried your childhood pain into adulthood. You carried critical messages that are still telling you, "I am not good enough, I am not smart enough, I am not deserving enough, I am not worthy enough." There is a constant inner critical voice undermining you, negating you, punishing you, creating fearful thoughts and feelings. As a result, you judge and blame yourself for your perceived failures.

When you think and feel badly about yourself, you believe that bad things will always happen, and often they do. You set yourself up to fail by believing that you will fail. You believe you will fail because it's blatantly clear to you that you aren't lovable enough or valuable enough or something else enough to be given what you ask for, hope for, and pursue.

You don't develop a solid inner core that can sustain positive feelings about yourself when childhood experiences have not been consistently loving or nurturing or when life experiences have not been consistently enhancing. You develop little or no ability to calm and soothe yourself. You do not develop your own strong voice that gives you messages such as, "I am loved, I am special, I am capable."

In order to meet the terms of your contracts, you can develop such unrealistic expectations of yourself, about who you think you're supposed to be and what you think you ought to be capable of doing, that you are doomed to fail. Alana's story is a good example of this type of thinking.

"I really did not organize my day properly and I am so angry with myself," said Alana. "I got my daughter ready for school, made lunches, dropped her off at day care, went to work, picked her up from day care, made dinner, cleaned up, gave her a bath, and read to her," said Alana. "But I didn't make the cookies for the Christmas party at her school the next day and I felt like such a failure."

Alana is very hard on herself. She has difficulty looking at where she is successful, what she does accomplish in a day, what a wonderful, caring, and loving mother she is. She is seeing the one thing she was too exhausted to do, bake cookies for her daughter's school party. And that one thing is how she is defining her day, and herself. Her contract is to be perfect in *every* way, the perfect wife, mother, employee, daughter, friend, and then she will be rewarded with acceptance, love, and attention. Alana often feels she is failing herself and disappointing others. The reality, of course, is that no one can be perfect, and when you strive for perfection in yourself or expect it from others, you will be disappointed.

Feeling Defeated

When you are repeatedly disappointed, it wears you down and you feel defeated. Your contracts never gave you what you hoped for. Phyllis feels like this.

"No matter which way I turn, there's a dead end," stated Phyllis in desperation. "I can never trust anyone. I am always true to my word. When I say something, I mean it or I do it. When I make a contract, I stick to it. When I finished high school, I wanted to go on to college. My parents said they would help me, and I believed them, which was so stupid because they never, ever followed through on anything they promised me. And of course, at the last minute, they backed out. They said they didn't have the money."

Phyllis continues, "My marriage fell apart after six years. My husband had an affair. I was devastated. One of the most sacred contracts I thought we had made with one another was that we would never betray our marital vows, our commitment to one another. I should have known this would happen. When we were engaged, he had had an affair. When I found out, I broke off the engagement, and he begged me to forgive him and promised this would never happen again. I believed him.

And now I'm stuck in a job that I hate. When I hired on, I was told there would be opportunities to move up in the company, but it's a dead-end job. They misled me and there's nowhere to go. What is wrong with me? It has to be something I am doing. I feel so defeated."

The something Phyllis is doing is *not* paying attention to the signals and red flags that have been going up all through her life. It's as if she has signed a contract to fail, by not acknowledging the messages in front of her that would give her the information about the pitfalls ahead. Having unrealistic expectations of others who are repeatedly unable to follow through on their contracts with you sets the stage for disappointment and leaves you feeling defeated.

You can't see how you get in your own way when you are unaware of the contracts you are adhering to. Your contracts have such a powerful hold on you that you continue to stumble and fall, create and re-create pain, until you figure out what they are. What is motivating you to perpetuate your experiences of defeat are the contracts, spoken, unspoken, conscious, and unconscious, that you have agreed to.

Exploring yourself

* Do you feel lovable?

* How do you set yourself up for failure?

* How do you get in your own way?

Repeating Negative Patterns and Themes

Repeating negative patterns and themes is the largest legacy you carry. You keep doing the same things over and over and over again hoping something will change, but it doesn't. You continue to repeat and replicate unhealthy patterns and themes when you are unaware of the contracts that are governing you. I can't tell you how many times I've heard, "Having grown up in an alcoholic family, I was determined (and made a contract) not to marry anyone who drank. So how did I end up married to an alcoholic?" You are drawn to what is familiar to you, even when that familiarity is your undoing. This is what Kimberly found herself doing.

Kimberly had a history of abusive relationships. "Why does this keep happening to me? When I meet someone new they look and sound healthy, but after a while it turns out to be the same thing."

"Do you think you could be attracting this to you?" I asked.

"What do you mean? Are you saying that when I walk into a room full of men, it's the unhealthy one I'm attracted to?"

"It appears so," I replied.

"But why do I keep doing this?"

With a history of having been physically abused by her father, it was not difficult to see that Kimberly was replicating a pattern. Though she made a contract to be the little girl she thought her father wanted her to be, it just didn't work for her.

But she kept trying and she keeps trying, in her adult relationships as well.

When what you are doing doesn't work, you keep trying to make it work. You don't have any different skills or tools in your toolbox to understand what you are doing wrong or how to change what you are doing.

Exploring Yourself

* What recurring patterns and themes are you aware of?

Becoming Physically Ill

As a psychotherapist, I see many clients who express physical as well as emotional distress. Headaches, backaches, high blood pressure, and chronic pain are physical symptoms that are exacerbated by emotional stress. Unattended emotional pain often turns into physical pain and is the body's way of demanding your attention. If you made a contract to deny your emotional self, and if you continue to ignore your emotional needs, your pain not only remains but is exacerbated and can become a physical reality. Your thoughts, feelings, beliefs, and reactions are not separate from your physical self.

Exploring Yourself

As a child:

* Can you remember a time when something upsetting happened and then you became physically ill?

As an adult:

* Can you think of times when you've been stressed and have become physically ill?

What helped you to survive in childhood may not be helping you in adulthood. What was adaptive for you then may be maladaptive now. The legacy of unhealthy childhood contracts is pain that you remain connected to in adulthood. You can change your legacies if you choose. You can release your legacies by releasing your unhealthy contracts.

Meditation

Begin a meditation. See yourself as the child you were. See how old you were. See what you looked like, where you were, if you were alone or who was with you. Notice how you were feeling. Now, see yourself as the adult you are at this moment. Walk over to your child, put your arms around him or her gently. Tell this child, "I love you, you are special, you no longer have to be afraid, I will take care of you from now on, you can trust me, and count on me to be there for you."

- Notice what and how you are feeling as the child and as the adult.

- Write about this experience. What did it feel like to hug the child? Was it comfortable? Uncomfortable?

Understanding This Exercise

Holding your child is a powerful exercise. There is no correct or incorrect outcome to this exercise. Rather, it serves as a measure of what your inner comfort level is around accepting love and what you struggle with. If you felt some anxiety during the exercise, know that this is normal. If you couldn't see the child, this too is something that happens for many people. If you could see the child but could not hold him or her, this says you aren't ready to embrace yourself. If you could hold the child but could not feel it, you are not able yet to take love in. If you could feel held and comforted, congratulations! If you could hug back, congratulations again. If, as the adult, you couldn't get to or hold the child, you may not feel you deserve it.

The importance of this exercise is to determine where you may be stuck and to learn to accept yourself. Practicing this exercise on a daily basis will help you to become more comfortable with the concept of giving and receiving love within and to trust that the love you give and receive is real, honest, and consistent. At first it can feel uncomfortable, unreal, and false. Eventually, it will be a powerful tool to use to soothe and comfort yourself.

Learning, Gifts, and Reinforcement

Write a paragraph about what you have identified and learned as a result of this chapter. What resonates for you? Where do you think you are stuck inside in terms of feeling deserving of love and why?

Write a letter to someone that had a powerful influence on your development. Tell that person how they affected your life, both positively and negatively, what happened as a result of this influence, what didn't happen, and what you would have liked to have happened. End the letter with, "I am writing this letter for me. I expect nothing from you. I want to acknowledge to myself my own thoughts, feelings, and experiences so that I can release the painful thoughts, feelings, and memories." This letter is for you alone and not to be sent to anyone. This letter is an opportunity for you to begin to free yourself from the connection to the pain you have carried forward.

What gifts can you take with you as a result of working on this chapter?

Practice the accepting the inner child meditation several times per day. Notice your feelings and thoughts as you are doing this. Write in your journal each day your experience around doing this exercise. You may want to rate how you feel on a scale of 1 to 10 as a way to measure changes.

Concepts to Remember

1. Your positive or negative contracts are a result of the belief system you integrated.

2. You saw your contracts as keys to your parents' hearts.

3. You developed coping techniques to help you to manage your discomfort.

4. Your contracts have left you with a legacy that may be hampering your ability to live your life fully.

5. It is important to practice hugging your inner child.

Chapter 5

The Healing Journey

Becoming Whole

Healing is the process of becoming whole. Emotional, psychological, and spiritual healing happens when you refuse to continue carrying your pain and make the choice to release your wounds. Healing has taken place when there is an internal state of oneness, a sense of inner calm and peace. The journey requires the commitment and the will to face your innermost fears. There are no shortcuts. This journey must be undertaken with the understanding that each step of the way presents you with challenges. These challenges are there to teach you important life lessons. Paying attention to and using these life lessons is essential if you are to successfully complete your healing journey.

Commitment and Will

When you make a commitment to anything, it means you are making a pledge. Making a commitment is an active and determined act. When you make a commitment, you make an agreement to something. Making the commitment to begin your healing process means you have decided that things are going to be different.

Having will means there is a drive and a push to fulfill the commitment. Will gives energy to the commitment. Both commitment and will are necessary components to change. You might make a commitment to stop smoking, but if you don't have the will to do so, the energy, the drive, or whatever you may call it, you will not be able to follow through.

Making internal decisions and adhering to them requires determination, persistence, and will. Desire is not enough, though it's a beginning. Will requires a summoning up of all internal resources to fulfill a self-promise.

Commitment without will, or will without commitment, diminishes the prospect of achieving change. If you commit to change, but don't have the energy it takes to follow through when challenged in some way, you will get discouraged and eventually give up.

Choosing to Heal

If you choose to go on this journey, you will gain insight into the powerful forces within that are either enhancing or undermining your life. Discovering yourself is a fascinating experience. Enlightening moments occur all along the way and you will ask, "Why didn't I know that about myself? How could I have not seen this, or understood this?" You wonder how you could have kept yourself in the dark for so long and are startled when the lights go on. Remember that you have to be ready to let yourself "see" what's going on. When things felt too difficult, you tried to protect yourself. When you were too wounded, you didn't want to inflict more wounds.

Now you have made the choice to change. Now you have made a decision to begin to open to the process of change. Now you have begun a new commitment, a new contract, one that will bring you to a place of internal comfort.

Making life changes takes time. It means letting go of what you have grown accustomed to. You know where you are now, maybe it's not great but you are familiar with it. If you let go, you may not know where you'll land. Change means taking a risk. Taking risks can be very scary. Making a commitment to developing a healthy self is something only you can choose to do.

Exploring Yourself

On a scale from 1 to 10, rate the following statements:

* I am committed to the healing process.

* I am willing to work at my healing process.

If you are below a 6, what needs to happen to get you to the next level?

Affirmation

"I *choose* to be healthy. I choose to be whole. I choose to be the person I want to be. I choose to create the life I want to be living."

Allowing Change to Occur

Opening up to the idea of change is liberating. You no longer have to be bound to sets of rules and contracts that imprison you. You can set your creative self in motion. Who you ideally want to be depends upon your ability to follow your own natural, internal flow. If you were stifled along the way by contracts that altered the internal compass you used as a guide, you got lost. You veered onto an alternate path that led you in another direction. This may not have been a direction you would have chosen had you had the opportunity to follow your natural inclinations. Intellectually, you might have tried to believe that this *was* the path you were meant to be on. Emotionally and spiritually, you knew it wasn't.

"Discovering Your Life Path" is a workshop I run for people who want to learn how to free themselves from the binding contracts that are limiting them. I have watched people transform their lives as a result of making a commitment to change and allowing the healing process to take place. This is Emily's experience in the workshop.

Emily came to the workshop because she felt stuck in her professional life. She was an educational administrator who was frustrated and worn out, but could see no other career path for herself. She believed that at age fifty-six, she was too old to make a career change and yet, if she stayed where she was, she knew she would sink further into depression. Throughout the course of the day, Emily discovered that her professional path had been predetermined by family expectations. She had followed the path her parents had put her on. She stayed where she was because she was still afraid to disappoint them, even though her father was no longer living. She saw herself as being "the good daughter, trying always to please everyone, but never feeling I could." She had never given herself the opportunity to discover what it was that she really wanted.

During the day, Emily identified her internal contracts, explored her wounds, made a commitment to breaking unhealthy contracts, and wrote a contract outline about what she wanted. "What I want," she shared with the group, "is to write children's books and to do the artwork for them." Her surprise was that, "I don't know where that came from within me. I came in today having no clue that this was what I really want to be doing."

Emily's Transformation

The Life Path workshop took place in September. The next March, Emily came to see me. She told me that her superintendent had offered her a year's sabbatical with pay. She was overwhelmed. "This is not something I ever expected. I don't know how this happened." I told her that she had made a commitment to allow change to occur. She had released her fears and her wounds and had given herself permission to break limiting contracts.

Emily did take the sabbatical, used it to write and do her artwork, and finished two children's books. She says she has never been happier in her life, because she feels free to be who she wants to be and to do what she wants to be doing. She no longer fears that she is failing others or herself.

Challenges to Change

What are the challenges to change? Everything! Change means that you are altering your life in some way. Change is scary, and the process can lead you to dark inner spaces that trigger uncomfortable or repressed memories. But the memories are there, even if you don't acknowledge them. Here is Jennifer's story.

Jennifer worked with me for a year and a half around her anxiety and low self-esteem. She had many trust issues and felt that her work with me had enabled her to begin to trust herself and others. In the middle of one session, she burst into tears. She was recovering a memory. The memory, repressed until that moment, was that when she was five, her uncle had sexually molested her. Jennifer was committed to the healing process and was determined to feel whole. In order to do this, she had to go through many dark moments and many self revelations. Her therapy affected all the relationships within her family. It took a great deal of courage to go through the healing process, but she chose to take the risk, and she healed.

Although the journey to healing can be arduous and challenging, the whole process does not have to be totally and utterly painful. Each layer of pain you release creates a space for something positive and healing to come in. There can be comfort as well as a sense of empowerment in the process of releasing pain in order to bring in joy.

Being Prepared

Knowing your commitment and level of will to enter into the healing process gives you information about where you are right now and what you need to do to get to the next level. Now you have to learn how to prepare yourself for thoughts, behaviors, and unexpected memories that might arise.

Sabotaging Yourself

Understanding your contracts and negative internal messages will help you to be more aware of undermining thoughts and behaviors. Though you may want things to change, you may sabotage that change without realizing you are doing so. Eleanore sabotaged her healing process.

Eleanore was struggling with depression and low self-esteem. She demanded that I guarantee her that things would be better if she did the healing work she needed to do. "Otherwise," she said, "why should I take the risk of opening a can of worms? Besides, I really don't think it's possible for things to get better."

For Eleanore, without commitment, will, or a vision of something better, change was not going to happen. She eventually dropped out of therapy, complaining that there was "no way things will ever be better for me." Eleanore wasn't ready to commit to change and was, in fact, fearful that the change that would occur would force her to make decisions about her marriage that she was not prepared to make. She had committed to coming to therapy. She did not miss appointments and she hoped for a long time that a miracle would occur. But her fear of what change would bring was more powerful than her ability to allow it to happen. I called several months after she stopped coming in to ask how she was doing. "Status quo," she said. "Nothing has changed. Nothing can change." For her, at this time, this is true.

Exploring Yourself

* How might you sabotage yourself, or undermine your effort, from allowing change to occur?

* How might someone else sabotage you?

* What are your fears about what change would bring?

Cycles of Pain

Holding onto emotional and/or physical pain can become a cycle. A common response to physical pain is a reactive tightening of the muscles. Instead of relaxing into the pain, you resist the pain. This creates muscular tension, which in turn, increases the pain. As the pain increases, the tension increases. You cycle into tension, then into pain, back into tension, back into pain.

The same thing occurs with emotional pain. When you are wounded, your tendency is to pull inward, especially when the response to your expression of pain has been non-nurturing. As you pull inward, you feel isolated and alone. When you feel isolated and alone, you feel more wounded.

You may have done everything you could do to deny your pain, push it down, drink it away, work it away. But it didn't go away. Your sad, fearful, angry, guilty, shame-filled feelings did not evaporate because you wished them away. Eventually, you accommodated to your pain and became so accustomed to feeling uncomfortable that this became status quo for you.

Acknowledging Your Wounds

Now it's time to become conscious. Now it's time to acknowledge and accept that you are wounded. It is natural to resist what is painful and difficult. Running away from your wounds was your attempt at getting away from the demons that were pursuing you. Shutting down gave you some relief, or so you wanted to believe. There is no longer anywhere to run. As the saying goes, "Wherever you go, there you are."

Being inside your wounded self, allowing that self to feel heaviness and sadness, is a difficult thing to do. Allowing yourself to feel your wounds fully is scary because your mind tells you that pain is bad, and if you stay inside it, you will never be able to leave. You want to get away from the pain and leave it behind. You want it to go away. You bargain with it to go away. These are the contracts you've made. "If I do something good, please will you go away? If I think good thoughts, please will you free me? If I resolve to stop doing this or that, please will you leave me alone?"

Facing your inner demons is the only way to release them and the contracts that go along with them. When you struggle with anything, you end up holding on more tightly. It is only when you accept and acknowledge that you are wounded that you can release your wounds.

Exploring Yourself

* What childhood wounds are you holding onto?

* How have these wounds affected your ability to trust others?

* How have these wounds affected your ability to be intimate with others?

* How have these wounds affected your ability to trust your own feelings and thoughts?

If you listen, you will learn something essential. You may finally face what has been holding you back. With this information, you have the opportunity to make a shift in consciousness. Once you can say, "I am allowing myself to feel the pain of my wounds," you make a conscious acknowledgment that they exist. Once you acknowledge they exist, you can see how they are affecting your relationship to yourself and others. You may feel uncomfortable doing this, but you are also empowering yourself by allowing yourself to see what you couldn't or wouldn't see before.

Affirmation

"I am ready to see clearly."

Ending the Struggle

When you stop struggling with your wounds, something amazing occurs. You realize that you don't have to let them control you. You don't have to be a victim of them. Ask yourself:

* Is holding onto my wounds useful in any way?

* Do I want to hold onto them?

The most likely answer will be, "No." What options do you have now? Could you think about releasing your wounds? In order to proceed on your healing journey, you must believe that not only do you *desire* to feel whole within, but you *deserve* to feel peaceful and emotionally safe inside. You do not have to stay in turmoil. If internal and external turmoil is what you are accustomed to, the thought of living without it produces anxiety. You ask yourself if you can ever be at peace inside. What would this feel like? Who would you be then? Is it possible to have what you want, need, or hope for? Do you dare to have dreams? Can good things really happen to and for you?

The answer is a loud and resounding, "Yes, you can be at peace, you can have good things happen to you, you can be who you want to be, and live the life you want to be living." But first, you have to give yourself permission to allow the change process to occur.

Giving Yourself Permission to Release Wounds

Choosing to release your wounds will allow you to begin to identify and let go of the contracts they are connected to. Releasing your unhealthy contracts will free you from the limits you have placed on your life. You don't have to hold onto anything that gets in the way of your being everything you want to be.

In order to make any internal shift, you must first give yourself permission to do so. Giving yourself permission means that you are aware and conscious, and ready to allow a process to occur. Until you give yourself the permission to release your wounds, you will hold onto limiting thoughts, feelings, ideas, and contracts.

You will have no internal space to incorporate and integrate a deeper understanding of yourself. You will continue to block what you want and need because you will still be holding onto old mind-sets and old unworkable contracts. What you think you want and being able to let in what you want will be in conflict. Are you ready to give yourself permission to release your wounds?

Without consciously giving yourself permission, you will block and sabotage change from occurring. To release wounds and to experience that release, you must be willing to give up what your wounds might be for providing you. For example, if you only received attention from your parents when you were sick, getting sick meant getting nurturing. If you find yourself getting sick frequently, you might want to go in and ask yourself if this is the way you want to continue to get nurturing and comfort.

Exploring Yourself

* Are you ready to give yourself permission to release your wounds?

* What do you gain by holding onto your wounds?

* What do you lose by releasing them?

On a scale of 1 to 10, rate the following statements:

_____ I want to be free of my wounds.

_____ I am ready to release my wounds.

_____ I am ready to let go of the connection to my wounded self.

If you rated a 6 or below on any of these statements, what would need to happen to get you to the next level? If you are determined to feel whole within, you need to give yourself permission to release your wounds.

Triggers

Wounds can become triggered and you can be brought back to the moment when you were initially wounded. Someone might say something that feels hurtful, you may have a sudden memory that comes up. When your wounds are triggered, you need to ground and stabilize yourself, and bring yourself back into the present. A way to do this when you recognize that you are being triggered is to focus yourself on the present moment and say things to yourself such as:

* It is now, not then. I am in this room (and describe the room).

* I am an adult, not a wounded child.

* I can handle this.

* I will be okay.

* I have not failed in any way.

Transitioning into a new self is not a linear process. Sometimes you will be aware that you've been triggered, other times you will return to the moment when you were initially wounded. When you do recognize you have been triggered and have grounded and calmed yourself, try to identify what has happened for you.

Exploring Yourself

1. Note what triggered you.

2. Note how this is familiar to you, how this replicates other experiences.

3. Think about why at that moment you may have been more vulnerable than at another time.

Triggers will always occur and there is something you can do to manage your reactions. Remaining inside of your wounds will block your growth. Releasing the connections to your wounds will clear the blocks and foster your growth.

Some wounds will never fully heal, and some hurts will always be a part of your being. This does not mean that you will never be whole. It does mean, though, that when you have been very deeply wounded and scarred, there will be times when you will feel exposed and vulnerable, and end up back in your wounded place. When this occurs, it is important to know how to take care of yourself.

The Real Goal

If "getting there" is the primary goal, then the journey has been only about reaching that goal. You have missed the moment-by-moment experience of life as a journey. You have been driven to get to where you thought you wanted to be next. Once you have what you thought you wanted, you may ask, "Is that all there is?" You look for the next marker in order to feed your need to feel okay.

You will never feel okay when you are trying to fit into someone else's model of who you should be or just by doing or having things. You can only feel okay when you believe that:

* Who you are is enough.

* You are doing what you're doing because you have made conscious choices that feel right inside for you.

* You don't have to prove yourself to anyone anymore.

You will feel whole when:

* You believe you are lovable.

* You believe you are deserving.

* Success is not tied to your ego.

* The journey itself has meaning for you.

* You feel peaceful and joyful about the life you are living.

The real goal is to learn how to accept, value, and appreciate yourself and your life. You can do this by releasing your wounds and all the unhealthy contracts you are holding onto.

Measuring Success

What standard do you use to measure success? Is success about how others see you or how you see yourself through someone else's eyes? What do your own eyes see? My definition of success has to do with how you feel about yourself, what feels right for you. It does not matter what anyone else thinks if you:

* Believe in yourself.

* Trust in yourself.

* Do what gives you joy, pleasure, and a sense of well-being.

If you can give yourself permission to be who you want to be, then you are successfully honoring yourself. You are practicing acts of self-caring. If you have loving connections, then you are successfully creating a life that has meaning and purpose. In order to travel on this path, you must make choices and decisions at certain junctures that may challenge you and cause you to experience feelings of doubt and fear. These challenges will be your tests. Do you have the courage, commitment, and the will to take the risks that are required in order to continue on your journey?

The Healing Process

The journey to healing is a step-by-step process. "When will I be done?" I am often asked. "July 10th," is my standard reply. My clients and I smile because, of course, I cannot give anyone a time and date when life will be okay. And the truth is, healing is an ongoing life process. You are forever growing and learning about yourself.

Life is a puzzle. You have pieces of the puzzle, large and small. The pieces are spread out, yet ready to form a whole picture. As you explore and understand more about yourself, you will be able to see which pieces fit comfortably into your new picture of yourself or which pieces need to be discarded. Are you ready to release those pieces that are no longer compatible with who you are becoming?

At the end of your work you will have an inner picture that fits with who you want to be as well as who you appear to be. Your work will continue as you go forward with your life and meet new challenges. You will have tools to use that will help you manage these challenges.

Getting to a place of comfort is rarely a smooth process. There are some people who forge through the healing journey. For most people though, the healing journey consists of fits and starts, moving ahead and falling back. The path is straight and curved, smooth and bumpy. Some milestones are easily reached, while others take more time because there are deeply imbedded obstacles that must be overcome. You might become discouraged when you feel you are stuck again and have reached a plateau. The journey will take whatever time you need to travel to your destination. You need to give yourself this time.

Taking the Time

Making inner shifts takes time. It takes time to awaken to yourself and to acknowledge your feelings, thoughts, needs, and wishes. It takes time to identify your contracts, patterns, and themes. It takes time to give yourself permission to release your wounds. And it takes time to identify who you want to be and what you want your life to become.

Trying to rush through the healing process actually delays the outcome and elongates the process. When you push too hard and too fast, you miss the messages and lessons along the way. If you shoot for the goal instead of the moment-to-moment learning experience, you will end up in the same place you started—feeling angry, hurt, frustrated, and disempowered.

Each step of the journey must be examined and the lessons explored. Integration takes its own time and must be honored. Years of hurt cannot be wished away or blocked off. You must learn to acknowledge your pain and your wounds, move through them, and then you will be able to free yourself.

Healing takes place when connection to internal pain has been released. The result is a coherent, connected, and healthy understanding of who you are. When a stable, internalized self evolves with loving internal and external connections, when there is an internal sense of peace and joy, the journey to healing has been achieved.

Exploring Yourself

On a scale of 1 to 10, rate the following statements:

* I am willing to work towards my future.

* I am afraid of being successful.

* I am afraid of failing.

* I am commited to taking care of myself.

* I believe I can create the future I want.

* I am willing to take the next step towards doing this.

* I will do this to please myself.

* I will do this to please others.

* If I get off track, I will learn from my mistake and try again.

Commitment Statement

I commit to beginning the process of healing.

Signature: _____

Date: _____

* * * * *

Meditation

Use this meditation as a grounding, stabilizing tool to help you to manage and release your wounds. Close your eyes and allow yourself to move into a relaxed state. Envision a sphere of golden light in front of you. You will be releasing any negative thoughts, feelings, and energy that you are carrying into this light. Allow yourself to acknowledge any uncomfortable emotions that you are experiencing. When you feel ready, give yourself permission to release the feelings, one at a time (i.e. sadness, hurt, anger, fear, frustration, guilt, shame, etc.). Breathe out slowly and allow the feeling to flow into the light in front of you. If you feel yourself resisting, allow yourself to accept that you are resisting and go back to being in the feeling until you are ready to begin releasing again. Let as much go as you are able to. Allow yourself to experience what it is like to let go of some of these feelings, even if it's for only a moment. Allow the light in front of you to hold and neutralize these uncomfortable and painful feelings. Move slowly and give yourself enough time to hold and release, hold and release.

When you have released as much as you can allow yourself to, envision yourself within a pyramid of white light. Breathe in this light. As you have released the darkness of the painful feelings, breathe in the energy of the light. This is a healing light, comforting, protecting, calming you. Know that you are safe within this light. Know that you are loved. Feel the energy of this light as it flows in through each cell of your body. Allow the light to cleanse and purify you. Stay in this light until you feel calm, centered, and peaceful.

Learning, Gifts, and Reinforcement

What have you learned about your ability to make and follow through on commitments? What do you now understand about your wounds? How have you held onto them? Are you ready to release them? If not, what needs to happen so that you can allow yourself to release them?

What gifts can you take with you from the work you have done in this chapter?

Choose a small, realistic goal that you would like to achieve. Make a commitment to working toward the goal. When making the commitment, write it down and rate it, so that you can see concretely what you are willing to do. For example, if you decide you need exercise and you like to walk, make a commitment to walk at least once a week for twenty minutes. This is a reasonable goal. When you are walking, use the time to relax and be in the moment of the walk rather than thinking about all the other things you could or should be doing. Notice when these could or should thoughts come up. When they do, take a cleansing breath, release them, and re-center yourself. When you get home, write in your journal the date you achieved this goal. Rate how you feel after achieving your goal. When you are ready, you might want to increase the number of times per week to walk or the time of the walk itself. If you miss the walk one week, examine what is getting in your way. Write down your thoughts and feelings, how you feel about missing the walk. If you were ill, for example, and in bed for a week, it would be reasonable that you missed the walk. If you sabotaged yourself, look at what you did and make a note in your journal.

Take responsibility for your actions. Understand that you can start walking again today. Failing to follow through one time does not mean that you have failed altogether. When you have achieved one small goal, you are laying a foundation to build upon. Then you can set another goal knowing you are capable of achieving any reasonable goal that you set for yourself. When you aim too high—like committing to walking one hour every day—you will set yourself up for failure. This is too ambitious a goal and not realistic. Choose a goal that sets you up for success, not failure. Make it reasonable. Change takes place in small steps. Begin with small goals and build to larger ones. Remember to pay attention to the moment-to-moment experiences along the journey. Celebrate your commitment to yourself.

Concepts to Remember

1. Healing is a process of becoming whole.

2. Committing to change is a pledge you make. Having the will to change is the driving force.

3. Making the choice to change is something only you can decide.

4. Allowing change to occur is challenging and transformative.

5. You need to prepare for change to occur.

6. Holding onto your pain limits you. It is only when you accept and acknowledge that you are wounded that you can release your wounds.

7. You don't have to be a victim of your wounds. You deserve to feel whole.

8. If your wounds are triggered, you can do something to ground yourself.

9. Success means you are honoring yourself.

10. The journey to healing is a step-by-step process and it takes time.

Chapter 6

Discovering and Developing Your Own Voice

Whose Voice Do You Hear?

"I don't think I know the sound of my own internal voice," said Valerie. "There are so many other voices in my head telling me what to think, what to feel, and what to do. No one ever listened to me when I was growing up. No one ever wanted to hear what I had to say."

Were you encouraged to express yourself when you were a child? Or were you always being told what you *should* be:

* Thinking

* Feeling

* Doing

If you were not encouraged to express yourself, you were deprived of the opportunity to listen to, speak, and honor your own unique voice. What you learned instead was to internalize, listen, and attend to the voices of others. These were the voices of your mother, your father, and other powerful people in your childhood. You believed the messages these voices gave to you. You based your contracts on the messages these voices gave to you.

If you tried to speak with your own voice and it was negated, you began to doubt yourself. When your voice did not match the external voices that were speaking to you, telling you who to be, you experienced an internal dissonance. What you thought and felt about yourself was not confirmed by what you were being told. You learned to value these other voices more than your own because you needed these voices to affirm you.

If you were not gifted with peaceful, gentle moments in childhood, reflective time, quiet spaces, permission to just be you, you did not learn how to tune in to your own inner voice. You spent your energies trying to quiet the discordant voices inside— those voices that made demands on you to be so very good.

Your true voice is that part of your internal self that acknowledges and speaks your true thoughts and feelings. Had you been given guidance and permission to listen to and trust this voice, the contracts you made would have been based on what felt comfortable inside for you rather than what you thought was acceptable or pleasing to someone else.

Exploring Yourself

In this moment, as you are reading this, what is coming up for you as you think about listening to and trusting your own voice? Are you experiencing a sense of acceptance, knowingness, clarity? Are you feeling fearful, anxious, or disbelieving? As a child:

* Were you given permission to express your thoughts and feelings? If yes, how?

* If no, what would happen if you did express your thoughts and feelings?

Giving Other Voices Power

If you were not encouraged to express your feelings and thoughts, you relied on the voices of others to inform you, guide you, encourage you, accept or reject you. When those other voices were negating you and belonged to people who were powerful to you, your voice was stifled. You struck your deals, lived by your agreements, and hoped everything would work out.

If you always listened to the voices of others, you never developed your own voice. You ended up giving your power away to others by listening to their voices, their rules, their messages. And you ended up feeling diminished and disappointed when you were met with disapproval, after doing what you thought these other voices asked of you.

"I finally told my mother that I was in therapy to help manage my anger," said Jude. "I thought she would be proud of me because I am taking responsibility for myself. Instead she said, 'Why do you always have to run to someone for help? Can't you figure things out on your own?' That really hurt."

At forty, Jude is still looking for her mother's approval. She still wants to hear, "I am proud of you." She is still trying to fulfill the contract that says, "I will do what I think you want me to do and you will give me your approval." Her history of failed relationships reflects and affirms the voice she carries within her. "You will never be good enough."

Exploring Yourself

* Whose voice was the most powerful to you when you were growing up?

* What did this voice tell you?

* Whose voice is the most powerful to you now?

* What is this voice telling you?

If you were fortunate, you were given consistent, nourishing, soothing messages that fortified you. You incorporated internal safety nets that you could rely on to catch you when you fell.

When something bad happened, you could hear comforting inner voices that might say, "It's okay. You're okay. You'll be all right. It's just one bad *thing*. You are not bad. You don't have to be afraid. You know what to do. I'm proud of you, I believe in you." The contracts you made encouraged and supported you, and enabled you to develop and trust your own thoughts and feelings, your own voice.

If you were less fortunate, then you were given harsh, critical, judgmental messages. You were left devoid of internal supports and found yourself feeling vulnerable and violated. You constantly searched for anyone or anything that might provide you with some assurance that you would be taken care of and would be okay. The inner voices you heard when something bad happened would say, "You are not okay. You won't be all right. You don't know what to do. It's another bad thing, because you are bad. You caused it, and it's your fault. You don't ever know what to do." The contracts you entered into in this case thwarted your ability to develop and trust that you were okay, and would be okay. You integrated all the critical voices you heard and your internal voice became a reflection of these voices. Who you really were and what you really felt and thought got lost in the din of all the other voices within. Your voice was ignored, or worse yet, silenced.

Elements of Struggle

The life choices you have made to this point are a result of the contracts you have made. Your contracts are based on whose voice you heard and listened to. Observing clients wade through their inner dialogues as they attempt to resolve inner struggles confirms how confusing these voices can be. This was Holly's experience.

After years of trying to "get on her path," Holly finally decided to go to graduate school. She narrowed her choices down to two schools. She was conflicted over which one to attend. "One will give me prestigious credentials, the other will give me more freedom to explore my eclectic interests and feels like a better fit."

Why the struggle? Holly grew up in a well-to-do family with expectations of excellence. One of her contracts was to "live up to my father's standards and then he would approve of me. He thinks I am irresponsible and a little flaky." If she chose the prestigious school, she would receive his stamp of approval. Choosing the other school would mean she was rejecting his values and choices.

Here's another piece of the puzzle. When Holly divorced a controlling husband, she made a contract that she would never again allow a man to make decisions for her. Holly was in a terrible bind. Her initial childhood contract, to live up to her father's expectations, and her later contract, to never let a man make decisions for her, were clearly in competition with one another and Holly felt she was in a losing battle within.

Too Many Voices

As we talked, Holly tried to explain what she was experiencing emotionally, and what she was working though mentally. It became clear that she struggles with who to be. "I listened to my father's voice, then to my husband's. Now I'm trying to listen to my own voice. I just wonder if I have the courage to honor it." Learning to listen to and speak her own voice and make life choices that feel "right" for her is a huge challenge for Holly, and very scary as well. When she speaks, she stumbles with words, apologizes for being unclear, and will then suddenly burst forth with thoughts and ideas that are filled with clarity and determination.

I asked Holly what school she really wanted to attend. What did her inner voice say? "I don't want to go to the prestigious school, but I don't know if that is a good decision." Until she can listen to and honor what her own voice is saying to her, Holly will continue to struggle and remain bound to contracts that are keeping her in turmoil.

Exploring Yourself

Close your eyes for a moment and listen quietly. Can you hear a voice?

* Is it strong or muffled?

* What is it saying?

* What does it say you need right now?

* Who does this voice belong to?

* What feelings came up for you as you did this exercise?

* What struggles did you have as you did this exercise?

When you begin to listen to your own voice, you will hear more clearly and more distinctly the struggles you have carried into adulthood. You will observe how you have been at war for years with negative and critical inner voices, words, messages, and contracts. You can then begin to speak back to those other voices so that your voice will be the powerful one, the one that is heard, listened to, and valued by yourself and by others. Though this voice may be meek initially, acknowledging yourself and practicing speaking this voice will eventually lead you to the path you wish to be on, rather than the path someone else has chosen for you.

Acknowledging Your Voice

Learning to acknowledge your voice is a process. You needed to hear positive, affirming, validating voices that said, "You are loved, you are important, what you feel is acceptable, what you say is important." Then you could internalize these voices. If what you heard instead was, "You are wrong, bad, a failure, stupid, unlovable," you created contracts that aligned with these invalidating voices. As an adult, you continue to negate your sense of self and you are filled with feelings of doubt, fear, shame, and confusion.

In order to counter this impoverished sense of self, you need to develop some awareness about what your inner voices are saying and what you are paying homage to. This means that you must learn to sit with what is creating anxiety, doubt, fears, and confusion. You need to stop running from your thoughts and feelings. What other choice do you have if you want to learn to develop your own voice, instead of listening to everyone else's voice?

Acknowledging your own thoughts and feelings is what connects you to your true inner self and allows you to hear your own voice. To know that connection, you need to learn to accept that what *you* think and what *you* feel are real, valid, and important. Not the negative voices of others that you have taken in and believed all these years. You have the right to your own thoughts and feelings. You may find that you are uncomfortable with what you are thinking or feeling, because of the messages and contracts you've made. Hear this. What you think and how you feel are who you are. In order to be able to flow into your true self, you need to believe, trust in, and welcome your own thoughts and your own emotional and intuitive feelings.

This means accepting what you like and what you dislike about yourself. You always have the option to change your thoughts and feelings, but you cannot implement this option if you are unaware of what is going on inside of you.

Exploring Yourself

* Can you hear a positive affirming voice inside?

* Whose voice is it?

* What does this voice say to you?

Affirmation

Begin to give yourself this affirming message: "What I think and what I feel are real and valid and important."

The Search for Approval

In chapter two, I discussed your need for approval. When you were feeling badly, you searched for approval or comfort. By doing this, you were in the precarious position of depending on someone else to approve of you. "If you like me, then maybe I'm okay." But what happens when you don't receive the approval?

And what happens if you do get the external approval, but your critical inner voice says, "It's not true, I'm really not good enough. You'll find out the truth about me." So it really doesn't matter who applauds you when you can't applaud your own self. It doesn't matter who believes in you when you don't believe in your own self. It doesn't matter how positive the feedback is when your internal voices are critical and defeating.

Giving Yourself Approval

You need to understand how crucial it is that *you* are the one to approve of your *own self* and that it's *your* opinion of yourself that is most important. Otherwise, you will remain stuck in the morass of critical voices that you have incorporated. As you learn to listen to and trust your own voice, you will become more grounded and centered within. You will gather internal strength that you can learn to rely on. You will come to know that your own voice is the one that is powerful and knowledgeable, and you will finally find some peace.

Brooke carries many voices within. She is a binge eater. She soothes herself with food when she is feeling bad about herself. "When I'm making dinner, for example, I hear the voices of junk food calling my name," she told me. "I know that sounds crazy, but food is a very powerful voice for me. Food says 'If you eat, you will feel better.' But I know I will also feel horrible. If I'm focusing on food, then I don't have to think about the other things in my life that are difficult for me. It's hard not to give in. There's a pain in the reality of my life that's in my mind and I don't want to look at it. How can I shut my mind off? I just want to stop thinking. All my voices are competing with one another for attention and I'm trying so hard to be as good as I can. I don't want to be in pain anymore. I want to find my own voice and my own power. I'm tired of spiraling downward and have decided that for today, at least, I'm going to acknowledge the things I do like about myself. And I am going to give my own voice the power to say no to the food. I have to do this and I have to break the contract that tells me to listen to all the critical voices that I have internalized, which have now become my voice. I don't want to listen to or speak with that voice any longer."

Exploring Yourself

* How have you searched for approval?

* Do you give yourself approval? How?

Affirmation

Say to yourself, "I approve of me."

Identifying and Developing Your Own Voice

You can't identify or develop your own voice until you can separate out all the voices within. You will need to develop an awareness of all your internal voices. So that you can learn how to discern your voice from all the others that you are carrying around. Can you identify and separate out all the noise in your mind? What you have been listening to and thinking about have become who you are. The voices and messages you hear have become intertwined with your own thoughts and feelings, so that you can no longer distinguish whose voice belongs to whom.

It is not always a negative to have internalized other voices. Developing a conscience requires that you listen to voices that teach you about good and bad, right and wrong, so that you develop a sense of values. Hearing a voice that is loving, comforting, and supportive allows you to incorporate these feelings about yourself. As a child, I felt very loved by my father. He expressed his love verbally and by his actions. When I am upset, I can still hear him saying, "I love you, Joanie." I use this voice to calm myself when I am upset. Incorporating affirming voices that encourage and support you is a good thing.

The point where the internalized voice becomes a negative is when it transmits messages that are inconsistent, confusing, and undermining. As a result, you create childhood contracts that validate these negative, critical voices and set yourself up for lifetime patterns of failure. Identifying and developing your own personal voice takes place in stages and requires that you spend quiet time in order to allow yourself to listen to *all* the voices within you and all the messages they transmit.

Stage One: Being Conscious

You need to be conscious and aware of your thoughts and feelings so that you can monitor them and counter the negative thoughts and feelings you are hearing. To do this, sit down in a quiet room and allow yourself to bring into consciousness a critical internal voice. Then acknowledge this voice—say to this voice, "I hear you."

Exploring Yourself

* Whose voice did you hear?

* Is this a voice you have often heard?

* Are there specific triggers that you are aware of that bring up this critical voice?

* What is this voice saying?

* Write down your reaction to this voice.

Writing down answers to these questions enables you to acknowledge the experience, make it concrete, and allows you to begin to develop an awareness of what is going on inside of you.

Stage Two: Listening and Acknowledging

Once you have learned to identify the voices of others and to separate them out from your voice, you can begin to learn to listen to and acknowledge your own internal voice.

Initially, this can feel very strange and uncomfortable. When other voices have been demanding and have been given so much power, finding your own voice can feel like an impossible and frightening task. It doesn't have to be. Think of this as the beginning of your new life.

Affirmation

Begin to say to yourself in your own voice, "I am worthy. I am important. I am deserving. I like me. I am lovable." Say this in the morning when you awaken and repeat this as often during the day as you can. Begin the process of listening to an affirming and approving voice. Yours! After a while, this voice will strengthen and the message will become more comfortable for you.

Stage Three: Developing Your Own Voice

Developing your own voice is a process and takes practice. Every time you hear an undermining thought or experience a painful emotion, you need to learn that you can respond to it. Rather than letting a more powerful voice control you and undermine you, you can counter and still this voice with your own true, strong voice.

If You Hear Yourself Saying:	**Counter with:**
I'm afraid that if I speak my voice, no one will listen.	I may have some fears. I can say what I need to say. I will be heard.
I think I know what I want to say, but I'm afraid I will loose my courage.	I know what I want to say. I have the courage to say it.
I can't get the words out, or they will come out wrong.	I can express myself. I can be clear.
I can't do this.	I can do this, I am competent and able.
I am bad.	I am not bad. I like myself. I am a good person.

* * * * *

Even if you are doubting yourself, doing this exercise repeatedly will help you to develop a stronger voice, and eventually you will begin to believe this voice. As you become more comfortable with your own voice, try speaking it out loud. Practice with someone that you feel safe with. As you practice speaking with your own voice, you will develop more confidence. Be patient with yourself. Remember that your goal is to be who *you* want to be, to say what *you* need to say, because what you have to say is important. Who you are is important.

Stage Four: Speaking to Others in Your Own Voice

Speaking with your own voice does not mean being aggressive or confrontational. Speaking assertively, clearly, and directly with your own voice is the way to acknowledge and express your thoughts and feelings. When you develop the ability to speak with this voice, even when it feels tentative, you begin the process of validating that what you think and feel have merit and worth. You begin to validate that you have merit and worth. You display to others that your thoughts and feelings are important and that you expect to be listened to. The purpose is not to control someone else. Rather, it is to assert your right to express who you are, what you think, and what you need. It's okay to ask for what you need. If you don't, you deny yourself the opportunity to explore if there is a possibility of having your needs met.

Even if your needs don't get met, you will have the experience of expressing yourself. Then you can look at who you are repeatedly turning to in order to have these needs met. If the person you are expecting something from is someone who has never been able to be there for you, what patterns are you repeating?

Exploring Yourself

1. Ask a person you trust for something you want or need.

2. Make it a simple request.

3. If they meet that need, thank them.

4. Acknowledge yourself for asking.

5. If they don't meet your need, still acknowledge yourself for asking.

6. Don't give up, try again.

Stage Five: Releasing Your Wounded Child's Voice

The path to developing your voice is littered with a history of rejection, fear, and hurtful episodes. Clearing out and releasing the negative connections to childhood pain will enable you to free your suppressed voice. One of the most powerful voices you carry within is the wounded child's voice that cries, "No one loves me, I'm so scared, I'm so sad, I hurt so much, why are bad things always happening to me?"

Without realizing it, you create situations and contracts that re-create and reopen wounds. Releasing your child's painful voice and developing your powerful adult voice will allow you to write new contracts that meet your needs in healthy, constructive, and enlightening ways.

Exploring Yourself

Make a four column list: A,B,C,D. In column A, write down something you are struggling with. In column B, identify whose critical voice is on one side of the struggle and what this voice says. In column C, write down what your wounded voice says. In column D, write down what your empowered voice wants to say. Here is an example.

A	B	C	D
Struggle	**Critical Voice**	**Wounded Voice**	**What I want to say**
Should I change jobs?	*Dad: "You will fail."*	*"I am afraid."*	*"I can change jobs. I will be successful."*

* * * * *

Stage Six: Trusting Your Voice

Trusting your voice is the next phase of the process. When you have had little or no experience accessing, hearing, or acknowledging your own voice, believing in and trusting this voice will be a challenge. How will you know if what you are hearing is really you and is really the right thing for you? How can you allow that voice to guide you, when it still does not feel comfortable to you? Here's how:

1. The more you listen to and speak your voice, the stronger it will become.

2. The stronger it becomes, the better you will feel.

3. As you feel better, you will learn to believe in and trust your voice.

4. One step, one day at a time.

Stage Seven: Staying in Touch with Your Voice

Once you develop your own inner voice, you will need to maintain a conscious awareness to stay in touch with it. When you stay in touch with your thoughts and feelings, you give permission to your own voice to speak your own truth. Listening to and respecting your own voice allows you to hear what you want, what you need, and what you value. When you cut that voice off, your whole self shuts down or detaches. If you don't value your own thoughts and feelings, no one else will either. If you don't listen to your own voice, you will disempower your voice. If you don't speak your own truth, someone will speak it for you.

Denying and ignoring your voice keeps you bound to someone else's voice. It is only by paying conscious attention to your own voice that you will have a shot at creating healthy, realistic, and positive internal contracts.

You Deserve to Be Heard

In order to overcome what limits you, it is necessary for you to let go of your undermining voices and the contracts that go along with them. Distinguishing your voice from others is a process. Whether it is your voice that you are hearing or someone else's, the important piece is, if what you are listening to is creating pain, conflict, and confusion, you need to counter and release that voice. When that voice belongs to someone else, this can feel like a terrible loss, because it might feel as if you have to let go of the very people who are most important and meaningful in your life. But that is not so. What you need to let go of is the belief that their voices, their words, and their messages are more powerful than your voice, your words, and your messages. Realizing that you have your own voice will be the beginning of the discovery of your true self. You deserve to be heard.

Your Empowered Voice

Acknowledging your own voice is empowering. Speaking with your own voice will be freeing. Acknowledging and speaking your own voice doesn't mean that you will never again experience fear and doubt. They are a part of being human. Everyone experiences fear and doubt at times. It does mean, however, that you will no longer allow these fears and doubts to limit, undermine, control, or even immobilize you. You will finally have the ability to counter the invalidating voices and messages of others that you have given so much credence to.

Exploring Yourself

Carry a small notebook with you. When you hear a critical voice speaking, write down what it is saying. Counter that voice. Write what you want to say to that voice. The point of keeping track of these experiences is to begin to look at whose voices are influencing you and to realize that your voice is the powerful one.

Meditation

Close your eyes, take a deep breath, and surround yourself with a healing light to protect, calm, and comfort you. Allow yourself to drift. Notice the voices that are coming up. As each voice speaks, identify who is speaking and hear your voice responding in the way you would like to be heard. As you speak, see the person in your mind stop talking, begin to listen to what you have to say, and smile at yourself. As you speak, hear your voice becoming stronger, calmer, and more assured. If you get stuck, take a deep breath in, and then breathe out and release your tension. Do this meditation for short periods of time until you feel more comfortable with your voice.

Learning, Gifts, and Reinforcement

Write about what you have learned from this chapter. What do you know now about the power of your inner voices? How have the critical, negative voices impeded you? What struggles have you identified that have followed you from childhood? What have you learned about your own voice? What first step are you willing to take to make your voice heard?

What gifts have you received as a result of what you have learned from this chapter?

In order to develop your own voice, pay attention to the other voices inside. When these voices feel uncomfortable and critical of you, speak back to them. When you hear, "You are going to fail," speak back and say, "I will do the best I can do and if I don't succeed the first time, I will try again." When you make a mistake and hear, "I am stupid," counter with, "I have made a mistake and will learn from this. I am not stupid, I am human and it is okay to make mistakes." Practice reinforcing positive thoughts and behaviors. Use comforting images, such as hugging yourself when you are feeling badly, as a way to soothe yourself. Begin each day with two positive self-statements and end your day with two positive self-statements.

Concepts to Remember

1. In your search for approval, you have relied on others to affirm you. It is your opinion of yourself that is most important.

2. Develop your own strong voice.

3. Be conscious of your internal voices.

4. Focus on listening to your own voice.

5. Practice speaking with this voice.

6. Respond internally with your own voice to a more powerful internal voice.

7. Speak out loud with your newfound voice.

8. Be patient.

9. Speak assertively, clearly, and directly.

10. Release your wounded child's voice.

11. Begin to trust your own voice.

12. Stay in touch with your voice.

13. You deserve to be heard.

14. Acknowledging and speaking with your own voice is empowering and freeing.

Chapter 7

The Growth Process

The Energy and Power of Your Thoughts

Thoughts are extremely powerful and generate a great deal of energy. When you have positive, self-enhancing thoughts, you generate positive energy. If you think you are lovable, you experience yourself as deserving, and are more likely to draw loving, positive people and life experiences to you. Your contracts will thus reinforce this positive inner view: "I am good and lovable and will be given what I need, therefore I can allow myself to trust that good things will happen."

If you have negative, self-defeating thoughts, you generate negative energy. If you think you are bad inside, you experience yourself as not lovable and not deserving. You are more likely to draw unhealthy, draining people and life experiences to you. Your contracts will thus reinforce your negative inner views. "I will try to be good, so that I can get the love I need, *but* that won't happen because I'm really bad and bad things will keep happening to me." What you think about becomes your reality. This is Paula's story.

By the time Paula was thirty-one, she had undergone a number of painful knee surgeries due to an injury that occurred in adolescence. She was single, isolated in her life, and had no vision of what her future would be, other than a continuation of her bleak present. Because of her history of knee pain, one of my first questions to Paula was, "What can't you stand?"

As a child, Paula had been sexually abused by her father. When she finally revealed the abuse to her mother, the response she received was, "If it happened, it was your own fault." So, Paula blamed herself for the abuse and thought she was "very bad," even though she tried to be "very good."

In therapy, Paula came to an understanding and acceptance that she was neither bad nor to blame for the abuse she experienced as a child. She learned about the mind/body connection and the relationship between her unresolved emotional pain and her current physical pain. She assigned responsibility for the abuse to her father, came to terms with the anger she felt towards her mother, and began to feel better about herself. She released her contract to "suffer and live with pain." She began to think about a possible future, one in which she was happy. It was at this time that she met a nice man and began a relationship with him. It is now ten years post-therapy and Paula is married to this man, has four children, and has not undergone any further surgeries.

Thinking Yourself to Health

This dramatic story illustrates how your thoughts become your internal voice and create life experiences. In Paula's case, the thought was, "I am bad and I deserve pain." This translated into years of self-blame for the abuse she thought she was responsible for and multiple painful surgeries she believed she needed. As she released responsibility for the abuse, and told herself that she deserved a life that was free from pain, everything shifted. She opened up to a loving relationship, refused further surgeries, and learned to live with a physical discomfort that had significantly decreased. In addition, she created the family she always yearned for. I marvel at the strength, courage, and commitment of this woman who has reversed a history of pain and transformed her life, because she was able to change her perception of herself and *think* herself to health. Instead of continuing to experience herself as a victim, she began to think of herself as a person who had the power to create contracts that would lead her into a rich, fulfilling life.

When you are able to recognize old, underlying, damaging, foundational thoughts, you can choose to release them. When you do this, you will make inner shifts that allow you to create new contracts that reflect your revised perception of yourself. As a result, your life choices and experiences will change.

Allowing Yourself to Grow

When you become aware of your thoughts, you will begin to experience your life differently. As your consciousness shifts, your responses to life's events will shift as well. Challenging situations that caused major reactions at one time may now be viewed as learning opportunities. As such, you give yourself time to think about how you want to respond to events and to people. You begin to realize that you have choices you can make about what you would like the outcome to be. You can be the driving force in your life rather than experiencing life as driving you. You are growing.

Personal growth is an internal process. It is a journey of developing internal awareness—emotional, psychological, and spiritual. Growth is about developing yourself to your fullest potential and being who *you* choose to be. Growth requires that you take responsibility for your thoughts, feelings, and actions.

Exploring Yourself

* Do you experience challenges as another painful life event to be coped with or as an opportunity to learn?

* Do you find that you are open to growth or do you resist it?

* Do you respond or do you react to challenging situations?

Releasing Your Fears

Fear is one of the greatest inhibitors in your quest to change. Fear limits your capacity and ability to function. It holds you hostage to your negative contracts. It keeps you stuck in undermining thoughts, feelings, and experiences. But if you let your fears go, you will be moving into unknown territory. If you let your fears go, you will be letting go of feelings, concepts, and beliefs that you have carried for a long time. And you are fearful about what will happen. Maybe you think you'd be better off staying with what you know.

What if letting go of your fears means you have to end a marriage or leave a job or disconnect from a family member? How do you walk away from something that might have some good parts to it? How do you know that what you are walking toward is any better than what you may be walking away from? Since you may not have made good choices to begin with, how do you know that the choices you might now make are any better for you? How can you suddenly trust your judgment? If you could just have a guarantee that you are making the right decision, maybe then you could take the risk of letting go of your fears.

On the other hand, what if you end a painful marriage and discover that you are still whole and are living without tension, anger, and hurt? What if you leave your job and find something else that fills you with a sense of meaning and purpose? What if you disconnect emotionally from a family member that has continually berated and hurt you, and find a great sense of relief, an inner sense of well-being, and a stronger sense of self?

Opening up to the belief that there is something better than the way you have been living your life, something greater than the limitations you have placed upon yourself, is empowering. Opening up to new concepts requires that you challenge your already challenged self. It takes time and effort to try to quiet the disruptive inner noises. When you are accustomed to experiencing fearful feelings, you are unaware of how much energy this takes. You find yourself:

* Pushing feelings in.

* Trying to divert yourself.

* Keeping yourself busy.

* Finding ways to anesthetize and protect yourself from your discomfort.

No wonder you are feeling depleted. When you allow yourself to look inside, to face your fears and release them, you will free yourself from the anxiety and stress you have been holding onto. You will find that your level of energy greatly increases and you will be excited about the future you are now creating.

Exploring Yourself

It's time to release your fears. Make a list of your fears. Using the golden light meditation from chapter 5, release your fears one by one into the light. Whenever a fear comes up for you, use this meditation.

Becoming Your Own Internal Architect

As you open and free yourself from your fears, you become your own internal architect. You draw new interior boundaries, design new interior landscapes, and add color and texture to your evolving self. What may have felt flat, dull, and hopeless internally can now be experienced as multileveled, bright, and hopeful.

Burdensome contracts that bound you tightly may be released and you can now redesign your relationship to yourself and to everyone else in your life. Your interior world expands as you relinquish your fears and infuse yourself with confidence and self-love.

Opening within and releasing your fears moves you along on your journey toward being your best, most complete self. Think about what it would be like to feel clear inside, to know what you are thinking, feeling, and wanting. When you release your fears, you will find you are:

* More comfortable with your thoughts and feelings.

* Looking forward to having positive life experiences.

* Letting other people in.

* No longer a victim of your life.

* Responding rather than reacting to discomfort.

* Trusting your inner voice.

* Making decisions based on your inner wisdom.

* Envisioning and creating your life as you wish it to be.

You can have all of this. It is not a fantasy. You can feel whole. You can *be* whole. The journey can be a joyful one. A writer recently told me that he did his best work when he was suffering. I asked if there was a possibility of approaching his writing with the joyful feelings he sometimes experienced. He said this was an interesting concept.

It's time to release those fears that are holding you back and redesign your internal self. What are you waiting for? Every moment of your life is precious and sacred. You are precious and sacred.

Trusting Your Instincts

When you have a healthy sense of yourself, your contracts will be empowering. You will know how to take care of yourself. You will trust your thoughts and feelings and use them to guide you in positive ways. You will be aware of negative energies and messages that tell you to move away from uncomfortable situations and you will be able to heed these messages. April's experience illustrates this.

"I wanted to take a workshop and called the instructor to get more information about it," said April. "During the conversation, I felt very uncomfortable about her. When I hung up, I had a strong gut feeling that I shouldn't sign up, but I couldn't figure out exactly why. I decided to trust my instincts and I didn't register. I am so glad I made that choice, because a friend of mine did go and had a very negative experience. I was grateful that I listened to myself instead of forcing myself to do something that didn't feel right inside. It reinforced that I could really trust my gut feelings."

April grew up in a family that encouraged her to make her own choices, valued her ability to assert herself, and applauded her independent spirit. Her contract was, "I can trust what feels right for me, and make good decisions based on this."

If you were not encouraged to trust what felt right for you, you could not develop an ability to trust your gut feelings, your instincts, your inner wisdom. Your contract read, "Do what you think others want you to do, because you don't know what is right for you."

Exploring Yourself

* Can you remember a time when you had a *gut* feeling about something?

* Did you honor that feeling? What happened?

* If you didn't honor that feeling, what stopped you?

Using Your Inner Wisdom to Guide You

Inside of you resides a very wise being. This being is you. Until now, you have not trusted in yourself, in your own inner wisdom. You have been the person you thought others wanted you to be. You haven't been sure of what was right for you. As you become more comfortable within yourself, you will no longer need to guess at who you are and if you are good enough. You will no longer need to do things in order to gain approval from others. You will be able to give yourself that stamp of approval. When you can do this, you can allow your inner wisdom to guide you.

The experience of being guided is an experience of trusting and following your instincts. When you allow yourself to receive and respond to your inner wisdom, the way in which you experience your life will shift. You will be approaching your life from a very different perspective. Your perspective.

Your inner wisdom is the deepest, most powerful aspect of your being. It has always been within you, even though you may have had little or no awareness of this. You did not know that you could access this part of yourself. Your inner guide is not complicated and confused. The messages are clear and when you know how to listen, you will get the information you need to guide you. Here is Bess's experience with her inner guide.

Bess's husband was diagnosed with Alzheimer's disease. He was able to live at home but needed her attention and care. Bess had a strong feeling that she should look at a new facility that had just opened that offered respite care for Alzheimer's patients. She said she didn't know why she felt the need to do so. Alan was doing well, but nevertheless, she followed her inner wisdom and visited the facility. Almost immediately, a family emergency arose and she had to be out of town for several weeks at a time, over a period of a year. Having a good place to care for Alan allowed Bess to be free to do what she needed to do without worrying about her husband's care. She says she is grateful that she knew enough to listen to her inner wisdom and let it guide her.

More dramatically, my husband's cousin had a strong feeling that there was something wrong within her body. "I couldn't explain it," she described. "I felt as if there was a time bomb inside me." Her checkup came up with negative results. She was not satisfied. She insisted that she be tested for a genetic predisposition for both ovarian and breast cancer. Her doctor did not believe there was a problem, but agreed to have her tested. The test results were positive and she was treated.

Your inner wisdom will always guide you in the right direction. When you learn to follow this wisdom, you will never again question yourself. You will have the ability to "check in" and determine what you need and in which direction to go. When something feels right inside, you will know that you have accessed your inner wisdom. Connecting with your inner wisdom is what allows healing to take place and growth to occur.

Exploring Yourself

Here is how to access your inner wisdom. Start with small tasks, such as whether to take a right or a left turn, whether to go to the store now or later, whether to make dinner or go out. As you gain confidence, you can go on to larger life decisions. Ask yourself what it is you need to know, then:

1. Release your thoughts.

2. Release your fears.

3. Ask yourself what would feel most comfortable for you to do.

4. Allow yourself to be guided.

5. Record your experience—did it work? How did it feel? If it didn't work, what do you think happened?

As you practice allowing yourself to be guided, it will become more comfortable and more natural. You will learn that you can trust your own decisions and your own choices. When you allow yourself to be guided, you release your internal struggles. You no longer need to expend energy trying to intellectually understand *why*. You only have to say, "Thank you."

Empowering Yourself

Feeling whole inside is empowering. Setting appropriate limits, being able to say "no" when that is what you are feeling inside, is empowering. Taking care of yourself in any way you choose is empowering. I give myself permission to have bed days. These are days, usually Sundays in the winter, when I don't get out of bed for the entire day. I read, I watch old movies, I nap, I may do some needlework. It doesn't matter what I do. These are days when I feel tired, when I need to hunker down and nurture myself. I've been asked, "Don't you feel guilty just doing nothing?" No, I don't. I feel great about myself, because I'm listening to my body and my voice telling me that I need to rest. If I don't take care of me, who will?

Listening and paying attention to your needs is empowering. Ignoring what you need is disempowering. Letting others control you is disempowering. It is not always *easy* to take care of yourself when you have been taught not to. Women find this especially difficult, as they have been programmed on so many levels to take care of others. You cannot take care of others well until you can take care of your own self first.

Speaking up for yourself is empowering. When someone negates your sense of what feels right for you, it is imperative that you clearly state to yourself and others:

* My feelings are real.

* My feelings are important.

You need to believe that what you are feeling is valid no matter what anyone else says or does. It takes practice to feel comfortable enough to do this. You must begin sometime, somewhere.

Empowerment Is Allowing Yourself to Be You

To be empowered is to believe in your ability to be who you are, who you choose to be, who you want to be. When you feel empowered, you exude an aura of emotional and psychic strength that is not threatening to others. You exhibit an energy that is clear. You stop, you think, you respond from your wisest self.

This does not mean you never experience fear. Fear is a part of life. You will have initial emotional reactions to life's challenges. What is different, however, is that people who are empowered don't stay in the reactive phase for very long. They understand that life can be fragile, that everyone can feel vulnerable at different points, but that does not mean you are powerless over your life. You do have the ability to decide how you will respond to situations, and this is what empowers you. You will have a stronger sense of self.

Exploring Yourself

* What have you experienced or done recently that has felt empowering?

* What have you experienced or done recently that has felt disempowering?

* Would you do anything differently? What?

Being Resilient

Being human means that you experience a plethora of feelings on a daily basis. You can awaken to feelings of joy or sadness and have no idea what your feelings are attached to. Your dreams affect you, whether you slept well affects you, what you project your day will be like affects you. Every interaction you have during the day has some impact on you. Your thoughts affect you. Your physical self affects you. People and things affect you. If someone is abrupt with you, this affects you. If your car breaks down, you are greatly affected.

It's amazing that you manage to function at all! The fact that you do function, and do so in spite of all you are subjected to, speaks well for how resilient you already are. This resiliency of spirit drives you onward, even when you feel you want to give up. Even when you get in your own way, you somehow manage to keep on trucking. Larry's resilient spirit enabled him to make significant life changes.

Larry had an up and down battle with alcohol. He experienced his life as overwhelming and felt he was a victim of his abusive upbringing. When his wife threatened to leave, Larry decided to go into an alcohol recovery program. After several months of treatment, his life view shifted significantly. "I realized how fortunate I was to have my health, my family, my work. I felt so much better about myself. I felt I was finally in control of my life, rather than it controlling me. I am so grateful to have realized what is important to me. I broke my unhealthy contracts and came back to the land of the living."

This powerful shift took place because Larry made a meaningful commitment to healing and had the will to follow through. He overcame years of pain and turmoil and created a life that allowed him to be who he wanted to be. He became a more present husband and father, left a job he was unhappy with, and started a business that he had always dreamed about.

Exploring Yourself

Let's look at how you have been resilient in the past and how you have overcome difficult situations. You may tend to look at your weaknesses rather than your strengths. It's time to turn things around and look at your strengths. Fill in the following columns with at least five items. They don't have to be huge life-altering events. Look at times in your life when you struggled with something and responded in a way that was empowering for you.

Difficult Situation	How I Overcame It
1.	1.
2.	2.
3.	3.
4.	4.
5.	5.

* * * * *

Are you surprised that you are as resilient as you are? Were you aware that you were so resilient? Begin to focus on what you do that works for you.

Affirmation

"I am resilient. I can overcome anything I put my mind to. I believe in my own power."

Learning Your Life Lessons

Your life experiences have been rich teaching episodes and the lessons, when assimilated, could fill volumes. Everything that has ever happened to you, everyone you have been in contact with, has taught you something valuable. Sometimes you were led to painful places and became angry. You wanted to know what you did to deserve all this pain. You resisted the pain and pushed against it, or you fell deeply into the pain and gave up your power to it.

Somewhere along the way, you need to determine how to use the pain as a teaching tool. There are lessons you need to learn, and when you are confronted with challenges, it is useful to understand that they are there to help you to learn something important about yourself and others. You may not like having to learn the lessons, but they are there for a purpose.

Until you learn your lessons, they will recur again and again. And each time you walk away from the learning, you will eventually come up against a harder lesson. When you keep repeating the same mistakes, when you keep ending up in the same dark places, maybe it's time to do something different.

Exploring Yourself

It's time to look at what is working in your life and what is not working.

What Is Working:	What Isn't Working:
1.	1.

2.   2.

3.   3.

* * * * *

Now, ask yourself:

* Is there a common theme in either column?

* In the not working column, what might you do differently?

* What is one step you could take as a beginning step?

Your life lessons are uniquely yours. You have gifts to be appreciated and you have areas of difficulty to learn from so that you can release what undermines you. Paying attention to the lessons you need to learn will free you from re-creating those files of pain. Every experience you have is important and valuable. How you react or respond to your life lessons is what measures how far you have come in your learning. Allow every experience from this moment on to teach you and guide you. If you do so, your world will be filled with magnificent rainbows.

Endings and Beginnings

You are on an evolutionary journey. You have begun a process of internal change. You have made a commitment to let go of what is no longer working for you in your life. In the book *Transitions,* (1980) William Bridges describes three phases of internal change. Phase one has to do with endings. This is a period when you relinquish an old way of being or doing. Phase two is a period of time when you live in a neutral zone. You are searching for definition and structure and are experiencing anxiety and turmoil. If feels as if you are floating and you are not sure where you will land. This is also a fertile, creative time when you are in a process of transformation. Phase three is the beginning. This is when you move into your new identity.

As you explore the contracts that are not working for you, you will be asking yourself which ones you are ready to let go of and what it will mean for you to do this letting go. As you approach the neutral zone you may find you are fearful and confused. "Why am I doing this?" you may ask. As you break a contract, you enter into a period of uncertainty. "Can I really do this? Who am I supposed to be now? What will happen to me?" You may decide you can do this and may move steadily through this phase. Or, you may get stuck in old doubts and fears and turn back. It is very difficult to let go of what you know. You may decide you are not quite ready for change and may need to regroup. The neutral zone is a time when you must find a way to sit with your anxiety. This is not an easy thing to do. As you evolve into the self you are choosing to become, you will create new contracts. You are making your way toward a new beginning.

Exploring Yourself

* What parts of your life would you like to let go of?

* What struggles do you anticipate occuring as you do this letting go?

* Imagine that you are living the life you want to be living. Describe this life. Describe what getting up in the morning feels like. What are you doing during the day? How will you spend your evening? Who will be in your life? What will be different about how you are living your life from the life you are now living?

* What parts of this life are you already living?

Meditation

This is a meditation that will help you to access your wise self. Put yourself into a relaxing meditative state. When you are ready, see yourself walking along a path in the woods. It is very peaceful here, quiet, calm, and safe. As you are walking, see in front of you a beautiful, clear lake. You decide to sit down on the grass in front of the lake. As you look into the lake, you will see a clear reflection of yourself. This is your truest and wisest self. Ask this self any questions that you need answers to. These answers will be given in the form of thoughts or feelings and will come to you now or later. You do not need to push. When you have asked your questions and received your answers, you will be given a gift that has some meaning for you. Ask for this gift and allow yourself to receive this gift. Take your time. When you have completed your conversation, you may get up, walk back along the path, and back into the present.

Learning, Gifts, and Reinforcement

What did you learn from doing the meditation? What questions did you ask? Did you receive answers? What were they? How did the answers come to you? What was your gift? Were you able to receive it? What do you think this gift meant?

Make a list of the life lessons you have learned thus far. Write about the spiritual gifts you have received in your life. When you are doubtful and questioning why things are happening to you, keep this information where you can easily refer to it so you can keep things in perspective. It is so easy to lose your balance when you are in the middle of stress and crises. Referring to your list of life lessons and spiritual gifts will remind you that life is purposeful and meaningful.

Each morning, before you get out of bed, make an internal list of what you appreciate about your life. Remember your gifts and say, "Thank you." Then tell yourself that you will approach each situation and each person you come into contact with today with a sense of calm and an openness to learning.

Concepts to Remember

1. Your thoughts are powerful.

2. Growth is about developing yourself to your fullest potential.

3. Releasing your fears will revitalize you.

4. Trust your instincts.

5. You are a very wise person.

6. Allow yourself to be empowered.

7. You are more resilient than you realize.

8. Every experience you have is a life lesson and there to teach you something you need to know.

9. Look at endings as new beginnings.

Chapter 8

Releasing Unhealthy Contracts

Why Break Unhealthy Contracts?

The contracts you enter into are based on your childhood experiences and are connected to your family's relationships. Though some contracts are healthy and can work for you, many more are unhealthy and can re-damage you. Your wounds are connected to your unmet needs and your yearning for love and acceptance. Breaking unhealthy contracts allows you to heal from the soul wounds that you have endured for so long. Breaking painful agreements is your pronouncement that you are taking back your power.

Breaking a contract does not mean that you have to be the opposite of who you have been. It may mean that you revise your approach to the contract so that it feels workable for you. For example, if you feel you must be the family gatherer, rather than to stop having your family over for holiday meals, you might reframe the experience and see that having them over is a gift for everyone. If you are the only one who will take on having family holidays at your house, you can choose to approach this day as something special you are doing to provide an environment and atmosphere of love, comfort, and nurturing. It means that you can be together and enjoy the experience of having and being part of a family on that one day. It can be an attitudinal shift that takes place and you may find that you look forward to the experience instead of dreading all the work and fuss that are involved. And you could ask for help with preparations so that you are doing it together.

Breaking contracts is about revising what no longer meets your needs and finding healthier ways to relate to yourself and others in your life. Breaking contracts is not about severing relationships but about discovering ways to heal and to build bridges so you can reconnect to your inner self and to those people in your life who are important to you.

Outcomes of Breaking Unhealthy Contracts

Making the decision to break unhealthy contracts requires that you identify and acknowledge the agreements you have made and are still bound to. These contracts that began in childhood have been an integral part of who you are. They affect every relationship you have ever had. There are few aspects of your life that have not been influenced by your internal contracts.

Breaking contracts that no longer work for you, that tie you down, that hold you back from being who you want to be and living the life you want to be living, is liberating. Breaking contracts, though, can and will challenge all that you believed about yourself and others. If you alter or break your contracts, you are changing the rules you have implicitly or explicitly agreed to. Each action you take will produce a reaction. This reaction might be positive, or it could be negative. There are two things that will happen when you break a contract:

* You will have empowered yourself.

* Something will change.

In order to successfully break a contract, you must be clear about your intent. Choosing which contract to break will depend on where you are in your internal process of feeling whole and grounded. Start with the simple contracts. Lay a foundation of success to fall back on when you need a reminder that you have done this before and can do this again.

How to Break a Contract

Now that you have done all the preparatory work, it's time to break your unhealthy contracts. Breaking contracts is, like everything else, a step-by-step process. Look at the contract list you made. Think about which contract you might like to break. Ask yourself the following questions:

1. Which contract am I choosing to break?

It's a good idea if the first contract you choose to break is a fairly simple and straightforward one. You don't want to set yourself up to fail by starting out with something that is too difficult or unrealistic. Here is an example of a simple contract. "I don't have to make my bed on the mornings when I am feeling rushed in order to feel good about myself." This contract could be based on childhood expectations about being neat and orderly and a way you gained approval. As an adult, you now realize you don't need to seek approval by making sure your bed is made. Breaking this contract involves only you.

The following is an example of a more complex contract. "I have to spend *every* Saturday with my mother. I have to do this so she will think I am a good daughter, and then she will appreciate me." This contract is more complicated to break because it involves another person and a commitment you made. Breaking this contract will involve a number of steps.

Begin with a simple contract that lays a foundation of success to fall back on when you need a reminder that you have done this before and can do this again. As you become more aware and experienced with what is involved in breaking simple contracts, you will be better able to break the more complicated ones. Only break one contract at a time. Otherwise, you will lose your focus and spread yourself too thin. It's hard to slow down when you want things to speed up and change. It may be difficult to choose which contract to break, when there is a list of unhealthy agreements you are wishing to release. When reviewing your list, you may find groupings of contracts that reflect the same or similar messages, so that by breaking one contract, you may actually be breaking several contracts.

2. Why am I choosing this particular contract?

Knowing where you are in your growth process can help you determine the contract you choose to break. A way to assess which contract to break initially is to review your contract list and determine which contract would be the simplest one to break. Later on, determining which contract to break will depend on what you understand about your limitations and fears and what you feel ready to do next. It's not a good idea to force yourself to break a contract that you are not ready to break. In order to be successful at breaking contracts, you need to have made the internal commitment to change and to have the will and energy to follow through. You'll need to feel settled within. This does not mean that you'll be free from anxiety around breaking the contract. You may be, but you may also feel some turmoil at the prospect of letting the contract go, and letting go of what goes along with any particular contract.

Understanding why you are choosing a particular contract at this moment will smooth the way for you. In your assessment, make a written list of the reasons you want or need to break this contract and what might happen when you break this contract.

3. Am I ready to break this contract?

Ask yourself if you are ready to break this contract. If you hear, "Yes," then go for it. On the other hand, you might want to break a contract, and may be on the verge of making the commitment, but you might feel you are not quite there yet. If this is so, then ask yourself, "What needs to happen in order for me to be able to take the next step toward breaking this contract?"

4. What do I really want to happen as a result of breaking this contract? What is my goal?

It is important to explore all your reasons for breaking a contract and to be clear that your expectations are realistic. Who are you breaking the contract for? Are you breaking it to meet some-one else's needs, to get approval, because you think you should do it? If you break a contract, will your whole life change, or just one aspect of it? Will you feel better about yourself? Do you have to break the whole contract, or is there a piece that you can change that will give you the effect you want? Is breaking this contract manageable for you?

Being clear about your expectations and assessing whether they are realistic gives you a better shot at achieving your goal. Breaking a contract in order to change a negative pattern for yourself is a realistic expectation. Breaking a contract in order to change someone else's behavior, to get them to be who or what you need them to be, is not a realistic expectation. Thinking that your whole life will change, that bad things will never happen again, is an unrealistic expectation. Thinking that some portion of your internal self will alter and as a result, you will feel better about yourself and your life is a more realistic expectation. Check out your expectations with someone you trust in order to get some perspective.

5. List all possible outcomes.

Make a list of all possible scenarios and consequences. Understand that you may receive some benefits from breaking a contract, but that everything may not be as perfect as you want it to be, at least at first. Determine what outcome is most essential for you. For example, maybe you ask for something but don't get it. How important is it to you that you have been able to express your needs? Does expressing your needs factor into receiving a positive outcome?

6. What is my plan?

In order to break a contract, or to make any change, you need a plan. You need to figure out what the steps will be towards achieving the goal of breaking a contract. Some contracts require giving yourself permission to stop a behavior that essen-tially affects only you. Other contracts are more complicated, involve others, and need to be approached gingerly. There may be many steps to take to reach the intended goal. List each step along your way, knowing you can modify the goal, the steps, and the outcome. Nothing needs to be written in stone. Things change, life happens, and what you thought might make sense for you initially may turn out to not make sense as you are on the journey to change.

7. What is my time frame?

It is useful to determine when you want to begin the process of change in order to ready yourself, to allow yourself to think about how to begin, and also to think about when you hope to have the task completed. You may alter or change both start and end dates, but at least this can give you a framework and a structure to work within.

Think carefully about what you want to accomplish by breaking your contract. Unrealistic expectations of when change will occur can undermine your commitment, will, and ability to complete the process. Change can be immediate, or it can occur over a period of time. It will depend on many factors, so the more you understand about what and who is involved, the better able you will be to be patient and understanding with yourself and with others.

If you decide to break a contract, understand that change will probably not happen all at once. Permanent change takes place over time. Building the foundational blocks to change will enable you to ground yourself and will give you the energy and the clarity it takes to proceed.

8. When I break this contract, who will be affected and how will they be affected?

Assess who, besides yourself, will be affected by your breaking a contract and how they might be affected. Though the purpose of breaking a contract is to take care of yourself, to be self-caring and self-nurturing, you do not exist in isolation. Your connection to others is significant and important, and you don't want to create dissension and disconnection.

Along with understanding *why* you are breaking a contract, you need to understand *how* breaking a contract will affect those you are in relationships with. When you approach life changes thoughtfully and lovingly rather than impulsively and harshly, you are more likely to achieve a positive outcome. Unless your intention is to sever relationships, and that may be what needs to occur, paying careful attention to your approach to others will enhance your relationships and your sense of self.

9. What are my fears around breaking this contract?

List the fears that are connected to breaking a contract. Understand what you are dealing with internally. It is natural and normal to experience fears around making changes. The more you can access internally about your fears, the better able you will be to release those fears that constrain you. Listen to the inner voices and identify their messages. Remember that it is fear that most limits you, so identifying your inner demons begins the process of freeing them.

10. Are any of my fears realistic?

Assess whether your fears are realistic. There may be real consequences to breaking a contract and you will need to decide what steps to take, and what contingencies to make. If you are in an abusive relationship, for example, leaving that relationship precipitously could be dangerous for you, and you would need to develop a clear safety plan. If your fears are not realistic, writing them down will help you to better identify this.

11. What is my commitment to breaking this contract? How willing am I to follow through?

How committed are you to breaking this contract? Rate on a scale of 1 to 10. How able and willing are you to follow through? Rate on a scale of 1 to 10. Go with the first message that comes to you. It's best to be honest with yourself, otherwise you will sabotage your effort. If you are at three, ask yourself what would need to happen in order to get to four. Do what you need to do in order to reach four, then ask yourself what you need to do to get to five. Getting yourself ready to make a change is as significant as the change itself, because it means that you are already in the process of changing.

12. How will I know if I have been successful at breaking a contract?

There will be different levels of success that you might achieve when breaking any contract. You might reach your ultimate goal, or you may achieve a partial win. Having realistic expectations, looking at all possible outcomes, and rating the different outcomes and what would qualify as success will be helpful. Successful outcomes can range from "I gave myself permission to take a day off" to "I expressed what I felt" to "I'm leaving my marriage in order to get away from a toxic relationship." They can be simple, or they can be dramatic. They can involve only yourself, or they can include others. Success might mean you are beginning to understand why you feel a certain way. A next step would be the ability to express these feelings to someone who is affecting you in a way you feel is hurtful. There is a whole range and continuum connected to success. You will know if you have been successful at breaking a contract, or beginning to do so, when you feel a sense of release and relief within.

13. What will I do if upon breaking a contract, the result is not what I had hoped for?

This is the risk that you take, and this is why it is so important to examine your motives, fears, goals, expectations, and approach. If you fail to achieve the desired outcome, you will need to reassess your situation. This will require a real ability to be honest with yourself, to really look within and see if you sabotaged the process in any way. Maybe you weren't really ready to break a particular contract, maybe you misjudged how you thought someone else might react, maybe your expectations were not realistic enough. Rather than feeling that you have failed and giving up, learn from the mistakes you made. Explore how you can change your approach the next time, what you will do differently. It takes courage to try new things, to take new risks. Give yourself credit for your courage. Pick yourself up and try again.

Failing is more about giving up than about trying and not getting it right the first, second, or tenth time. Each attempt will teach you something about how to fine-tune your approach. You fail when you repeat the same negative patterns that don't work and refuse to look at what you are doing. Then you remain stuck and eventually give up on yourself and on others as well.

14. At what point do I evaluate the process?

Evaluation and re-evaluation needs to take place all along the way, because as things shift, so might your goal. You may decide to stop the process because you are not ready, you may decide to limit your goal, you may decide to expand your goal, or you may decide to go in a whole other direction. Months after breaking your contract and achieving your goal, it will be important to review what you have learned. Each achievement or attempt is a learning experience and helps to build upon the foundation you have established. When you are doubting yourself, and you will certainly have this experience at times, you can look back on what you have learned, where you have grown, and use this learning to re-center and re-ground yourself.

Pulling It All Together

Once you have decided to break a particular contract and have evaluated the ways in which it will affect both you and others, there are different approaches you may want to assess. Each contract will be different and will need to be addressed individually. Using the following examples, let's go through them to see how breaking a contract might be approached.

This contract involves only one person, Susan. Let's go through the steps with how the questions were answered by her:

Susan's Contract

1. What contract am I choosing to break?

   The contract I choose to break is: I have to be perfect, I can't make mistakes.

2. Why am I choosing this particular contract?

   I feel stressed and pressured all the time.

3. Am I ready to break this contract?

   Yes.

4. What do I want to happen as a result of breaking this contract? What is my goal?

   I want to be less demanding of myself, more accepting with myself and everyone else in my life.

5. Possible outcomes:

   I could let go of my need to be perfect and feel great. I could struggle and try to let go, not be able to, and feel awful about myself. I could do a little letting go at a time. I could let go of everything at once and make a real mess.

6. What are the steps I need to take?

   I will use affirmations that tell me I don't have to be perfect, that it's okay to make mistakes. I will not berate myself when I think something is not perfect. I will be forgiving with myself.

7. What is my time frame?

   I will begin today.

8. When I break this contract, who will be affected and how will they be affected?

   Certainly I will be significantly affected. And I think this will affect the people in my life that feel I'm too demanding with them.

9. What are my fears around breaking this contract?

   That if I'm not perfect, people will not like me.

10. Are any of my fears realistic?

    No, except maybe with my parents. But I'm ready to be who I want to be.

11. What is my commitment to breaking this contract on a 1 to 10 scale? How willing am I to following through on a 1 to 10 scale?

    8 for commitment and will.

12. How and when will I know if I have been successful at breaking this contract?

    I will be more relaxed and at ease with myself. I know it will take some time to get used to. I'll evaluate in a month.

13. What will I do if, upon breaking this contract, the result is not what I had hoped for?

    Then I'll look to see if I was really ready to let go of my contract, how I approached my process, and try again.

* * * * *

Here's a more complicated contract filled out by Scott that involves other people.

Scott's Contract

1. Which contract am I choosing to break?

   The contract I choose to break is: I must work very hard and I must run the family business the way my father expects me to.

2. Why am I choosing this particular contract?

   I need to free myself from feeling that I am disappointing everyone by trying to meet other people's expectations. I want to feel that I have some power to choose what I think is important for me. I want to spend more time with my family and less time at work.

3. Am I ready to break this contract?

   I think I am.

4. What do I really want to happen as a result of breaking this contract? What is my goal?

   I want to have a better relationship with my wife and son, and for them to know that I love them very much. I don't want to be so tied to the business, and I want my father to accept that my family is important to me and to not be angry with me for making time for my family on weekends. I want my brother, who is my business partner, to understand and accept this as well.

5. Possible outcomes:

   Dad and Jim will understand. Dad will understand and Jim won't or vice versa. I could back out because I'm too scared. I could alienate my dad and Jim. If I screw it up, my wife will be angry and so will my son. I will speak my own voice and that will be a good beginning for me. I could work at negotiating with my dad and Jim. Maybe I could work some weekends and take some off. Maybe Jim would like to take some weekends off too.

6. What steps do I need to take? What is my plan?

   I will speak to Dad first and let him know that I respect his feelings about the business but I feel differently and hope he can understand this. I will tell him that the business is important to me as well, but my wife and son need to feel that they are important to me. Then I will speak with Jim and tell him the same thing and ask that he accept and

understand my feelings. If he is upset or angry, I will tell
him that I am sad that he can't understand how I feel.

7. What is my time frame?

   I will talk to Dad and Jim within the next two weeks.

8. When I break this contract, who will be affected and how
   will they be affected?

   My son and wife will be affected. They will know that they
   come first in my life. Dad will be affected. He will see that
   I have changed my priorities. He might be angry or
   disappointed in me. Jim will be affected because I want to
   spend less time at work and he may feel he has to take
   on more responsibility. He might feel I am deserting him. I
   hope he will be okay with it.

9. What are my fears around breaking this contract?

   That my father and brother will be angry with me and that
   I won't be able to follow through on my commitment to my
   wife and son.

10. Are any of my fears realistic?

    Yes. Everyone could feel angry with me and I could feel
    guilty. I guess it depends on how I handle things, what I
    feel I am ready for, and how much I want to feel that I am
    in control of my own life.

11. What is my commitment to breaking this contract on a 1 to
    10 scale? How willing am I to follow through on a 1 to 10
    scale?

    10 for commitment, 7 for will.

12. How and when will I know if I have been successful at
    breaking this contract?

    I will know that I have succeeded if I actually can speak
    up to Dad and to Jim and tell them clearly that I want
    more time with my family and less time at the business,
    and if I do spend more time with my family.

13. What will I do if, upon breaking this contract, the result is not what I had hoped for?

    I will feel really bad. I will need to keep trying to work on myself and on my relationships with everyone. At least I will know that I am making an attempt to change a difficult situation. Maybe one thing will happen that will be good, and then I can work on the next thing.

*   *   *   *   *

Scripting

The contract model provides a structure within which you can explore your thoughts, feelings, and actions. You may come up with additional questions and ideas for sorting through difficult situations and decisions as you process your answers. As you answer one question, you may find yourself reaching some other conclusions that you can go back and explore more fully. This model can serve as a sort of script you can use to proceed. It is helpful to write out what you want to say to someone and rehearse it so that you are clear about what it is you want to happen and don't get stuck or tongue-tied.

My Contract

1. What contract am I choosing to break?

2. Why am I choosing this particular contract?

3. Am I ready to break this contract?

4. What do I really want to happen as a result of breaking this contract? What is my goal?

5. List all possible outcomes.

6. What steps do I need to take? What is my plan?

7. What is my time line?

8. When I break this contract, who will be affected and how will they be affected?

9. What are my fears around breaking this contract?

10. Are any of my fears realistic?

11. What is my commitment to breaking this contract on a 1 to 10 scale? How willing am I to following through on a 1 to 10 scale?

12. How and when will I know if I have been successful at breaking this contract?

13. What will I do if, upon breaking this contract, the result is not what I had hoped for?

14. Evaluate.

* * * * *

Contract Release

Write out the contract you are choosing to release. When you have gone through the steps and are ready to release this contract, complete the following.

Contract

_____

_____

_____

Date: _____

I, _____, release the above contract.

Signature: _____

* * * * *

Meditation

See yourself sitting on one side of a doorway that has a golden curtain separating two rooms. On the other side of the doorway, visualize someone you have given your power to. Visualize this person holding a ball. This ball represents your power. How large is the ball? Gently reach through the doorway and take the ball through the doorway and hold it on your lap. This is a way to take your power back. Once you have taken your power back, notice the size of the ball.

Learning, Gifts, and Reinforcement

What was the experience of breaking a contract like for you? What was difficult? What was comfortable? How might you approach the process of breaking your next contract differently? What did you like about it? What did you dislike? What created anxiety? What positive feelings did you experience?

What gifts can you take with you as a result of having broken a contract?

Practice the meditation around taking your power back as many times a day as you can. You have given your power to others hoping that you would receive what you needed and wanted. It is time to give to yourself what you need and want. Experience yourself as powerful, rather than as powerless. Know that you are the victor rather than the victim. Love yourself to a higher level of being. Break those contracts that contradict your new promise to yourself to be whole.

Concepts to Remember

1. Breaking unhealthy contracts allows you to heal.

2. Breaking unhealthy contracts is liberating and empowering.

3. Breaking unhealthy contracts is a step-by-step process.

4. Breaking unhealthy contracts releases you from the pain of your soul wounds.

Chapter 9

Creating New Contracts

Where You Are

Breaking unworkable contracts leads you to the next step of rewriting these contracts so they fit who you have become and who you want to be. Creating new contracts is another process that must be done thoughtfully and carefully. Creating new contracts at this stage is different than the first time around, when contracts were based on childhood messages. At that time, you were not aware that you were making internal agreements. Your contracts were based on your need for approval, love, acceptance, and validation.

Now you are more in touch with who you are and who you want to be. Now you can decide to create new contracts that are based on your new, healthy self. You can now write contracts that are enhancing to you and your relationships with others. You are learning how to respond rather than react to inner drives and external demands, and to evaluate what is possible, reasonable, and healthy for you. You have the benefit of hindsight. You know what has not worked. You know where you have been stuck. You know what forces have limited you. You understand more deeply and clearly the inner voices that have deterred you, and you are better at hearing and understanding your own true voice.

You have explored the ways in which you sabotage yourself, and you know on a deeper level what is in your heart and soul, what feeds and nurtures you. Hopefully, your growing compassion towards yourself and others has led you to a more peaceful place within. You have a more defined sense of self and a clearer vision of what you need and want.

You have challenged yourself and must understand that you will always be challenged in this life. This is such an important concept to understand. What can get easier is how you manage the challenges and how you empower yourself, so that you do not experience yourself as a victim.

The Importance of Creating New, Healthy Contracts

Creating new contracts is an important part of taking responsibility for meeting your challenges and asserting that you have power. You have the power to generate whatever you need in order to make your life not only work for you, but also to allow yourself to continue to blossom and to grow in the direction of your choosing. Creating new contracts is a choice that you can make because you have decided that no longer will you have agreements imposed on you. No longer will you acquiesce to the voices of others. Rather, you will meet these voices head on, face them, and release those that thwart you in any way. You will design your own present and future from now on.

Creating new contracts can involve making simple decisions or it can be a multistep process. This will depend on what the situation is, where you are emotionally at the moment, and who else might be involved or affected. Whether simple or complicated, the contracts you write from this point on will be done consciously and purposefully to enhance and benefit you in healthy ways.

Visualizing

Writing new contracts requires the same attention to detail as breaking old contracts. It's important to know what you don't want. It's just as important to know what it is that you do want, because otherwise you won't create it. To say, "I don't want to be in this relationship the way it is any longer," does not create the picture of how you want this relationship to look, feel, and be. Creating the vision is as important as letting go of the experience that isn't working for you. Visualizing is an essential part of the process of creating new contracts. Seeing what you want to happen puts things into motion and puts you in charge of developing new ways of being, thinking, and doing.

When you visualize what you want to happen in your life, you send out energy. Remembering that thoughts create experiences, what you envision, consciously and unconsciously, is likely to manifest. Visualizing is the ability to imagine. Imagining is a creative process. Learning to be conscious and focused and to decide what it is you want unleashes your creativity. When you are ready to visualize, you are ready to create.

Exploring Yourself

To visualize what you want, sit in a quiet place and think about what it is that you want to manifest. Use the following guidelines:

* Don't ask for others to change into who you need them to be. You cannot change a relationship by wishing someone else will change. You can only change the way in which you participate in that relationship.

* Don't ask for anything that will impact someone else negatively.

* Don't ask for more than you need.

* Do ask for insight about what you need to do so that you can accept or let go of what is not right for you or who is not right for you.

* Do ask for what will bring you to your best self. Anything is possible when you are ready and open.

* Begin with something small.

* Write down what you want to happen in as much detail as possible.

- Then, visualize what you want to happen, being clear and specific. Create a moment-to-moment experience. For example, "I see myself waking up at 7 A.M. I get out of bed, take a shower, and get ready for the day. I am in my car driving to my new job. I walk into the building and greet my coworkers. I see myself at my desk, doing a graphic design for a new brochure that I am creating for the company. I am excited about this project." The more specific your visualization is, the better.

- Go within and check to see if there are any underlying fears or doubts. If there are, release them into the golden light. Then go back and visualize what you want to happen.

- Re-create this vision over and over and stay clear with it. Practice patience. Along with creating the vision, you will need to participate in helping it along.

- Visualizing is fun and empowering because you are imagining what you want to occur. If you visualize something and it does not occur, it is important to then know that this may not be what needs to happen. You may not be ready, this may not be the right time, or it may not be in your best interest. Then you can regroup and rethink your process or your vision. You are in charge of your life and your vision. When you want to enter into anything new, begin to utilize the visualizing process so that you have clarity and can create what it is you want to happen.

Being Reality Based

You may visualize whatever you choose, but you may receive only a part of what you wanted. Then you are going to need to come to terms with this in some way. What you yearn for may be the ideal, what you can have might be somewhere in-between. That does not mean that you can't have what you want, or shouldn't dare to dream of the ideal. It does mean that you need to inject some reality into your vision. When you are in the process of developing a new contract, you need to think carefully about what you specifically want to happen. Wanting something and having that something materialize is not just a magical occurrence. You must participate in the process of the creation. As part of that process, you need to see what is possible and achievable. For example, you may want to write a new contract that states:

> I will no longer do anything for anyone else. I'm tired of trying to get love and appreciation. I don't care anymore. The hell with them all.

Recognize that this is coming from a place of hurt and anger. This could create a great deal of conflict and disharmony internally and with others, because you are abruptly cutting off avenues for resolution. A more thought-out and worked-out contract might state:

> From now on, when someone asks something of me, I will think about what feels comfortable and will give myself time to think about it. If it's something I'm uncomfortable with, I will know that it's okay to talk it over with them and see if we can work it out. In this way, I am respecting myself and my needs and I am acknowledging that I do not have to do everything that's asked of me in order to receive love.

With this contract, you are not reacting out of anger and hurt. You have given yourself time to process what will work for you; you can negotiate with others about what is comfortable and workable for you. You are also sending a clear message that you respect yourself and you are not afraid of losing love or friendship. This is the most important message you can give to yourself and send to others. If, as a result of this new contract, someone does reject you because you won't do what they want you to do, you will be better able to respond from a more grounded place. It also means that you will no longer allow yourself to be manipulated into doing what no longer feels right for you because you need approval at any cost.

When you decide to break a contract and to rewrite it, you are making a decision to change some *thing* or some *way* you have been but choose no longer to be. And when you do this, you must be as careful, thoughtful, and kind to yourself, and do what feels reasonable within you. Sometimes you are kinder and more considerate of others than you are to your own self. Pay attention to what feels right for you.

Brainstorming

Begin thinking about the new contract you want to write. Use the following guide:

* Understand what your needs are and what it is you want to happen.

* Clearly define what you want the outcome to be.

* Be aware that there are different approaches you might take.

* Ask yourself how you will be affected by rewriting a contract and what will change for you.

* Try to take into account how other people might be affected by your new contract. Think about how you might feel if you were in their situation. This puts you in their position and might allow you to understand where they may be coming from. If you can address this verbally, it might lead to a better understanding. You might not be able to meet their needs, but acknowledging lets them know you hear them and understand that their needs are important to you as well as to them. This may not always be possible to do. You can only do your best.

Until you feel comfortable with what you really want, you won't be able to rewrite your contract or be clear that it is going to work for you. Taking care of yourself by understanding your needs can result in successfully breaking and re-writing a contract on your terms rather than acquiescing to your own unrealistic expectations or someone else's terms.

Writing Your New Contract

This is the icing on the cake. This is where you get to create your future in a real way. Writing new contracts is a powerful experience. You have identified what is no longer working for you and why it no longer works for you. You have made a decision to heal and to get on a new path. You have cleared the blocks that limit you, or are in the process of doing so.

Creating new contracts puts you in charge of the rest of your life. All of the decisions you make from this point forward are conscious ones. You will need to continually check in and explore hidden agendas, undermining thoughts, and painful trigger points. Life is a continual process of having underlying data revealed. This data comes up when you least expect it.

Just when you think you have come to a place of peace and understanding within, you can be powerfully jolted and surprised to find yourself reacting strongly to a thought, a feeling, what someone says or does, a movie, a song, etc. This happens because there are so many layers within that need to be brought into consciousness. This is definitely not a bad thing and need not be viewed as discouraging. Rather, when something you need to see comes up, recognizing it is there to teach you something will be a great learning experience. You are learning where it is you still need to grow. Your learning is never-ending. You will never know it all.

Rewriting your contracts leads you into the next phase of your life. This process requires care and attention. The end result can be a new beginning, a transformed self, and a joyous life experience. You have stepped out of what binds and constricts you, and you are now giving yourself the opportunity to step into the rest of your life.

The Steps to Creating New Contracts:

1. Scale the following statements from 1 to 10:

_____ I am afraid of being successful.

_____ I am afraid of failing.

_____ I am committed to creating a new contract.

_____ I can create the future I want.

_____ I am willing to take the next step towards doing this.

_____ I will do this to please myself.

_____ I will do this to please others.

_____ If my new contract doesn't work, I will learn from my mistakes and try again.

It is essential to understand where you are at this point, what you are able to commit to now, and what you may still be struggling with. Be honest with your answers. No one but you will see them. No one but you can initiate the process of change, so the more honest you are with yourself, the better able you will be to evaluate where you are in the moment. If most of your answers are less than 7, you will need to go back and do more work around getting yourself ready to rewrite your contracts. You might be ambivalent because your fears may come into play about what change will mean for you. This is understandable, but don't allow your fears to undermine your progress. Accept that you have some fears around change, go inside and comfort yourself, then take the next step towards healing and moving forward.

2. Write out your old contract:

_____

_____

_____

3. Sign a commitment statement:

I commit to creating a new life experience.

Signature: _____ Date: _____

4. Visualize what you want to happen as a result of rewriting your contract.

Be clear and specific. Ask yourself if you are sure that's what you really want. Be sure that what you want is not just about getting applause and approval. Set your sights on what will be for your highest good. Remember, it's about you and is not about controlling or changing anyone else.

5. Write out a contract outline.

The outline presents the details for what you want to achieve and names the steps you will be taking in order to reach your goal. Write an outline that is specific about what you want as an outcome, what you hope to achieve. Choose a goal that is accomplishable and important to you. Use action-oriented words. Here are some examples:

Emily's Contract Outline:

My need is to let my protective walls down so I can feel less isolated and have more connection in my life.

This is a generalized statement, because there are no guidelines as to how the goal will be met, who will be affected, how Emily will engage in the process, or what steps she will be taking. Without a well-defined statement, the outcome will most likely be unsatisfactory. It is important to know your needs and to then be able to concretely verbalize your process.

Emily's Revised Contract Outline:

My need is to stop being so afraid that I will be hurt if I open myself up to other people. I want to feel and believe that I am deserving of love and affection from others and that I can trust others. I will begin by practicing my affirmations. I will start bringing people into my life. I will ask Helen at work to have lunch with me. I will join the book club at the library as a way to begin meeting new people. I will ask my brother if he wants to go to a movie. When I do these things, I will feel less alone and less isolated in my life. I will build a life that has more connection with others.

This contract outline is more concisely developed. It states a goal, who will be affected, a specific plan of action, and an outcome statement. This statement is more encompassing and inclusive. There is a higher probability with this outline; the new contract will be more achievable.

6. Write out your new contract using the contract outline.

In the above case, it would read:

I no longer need to be afraid that I will be hurt. I will begin to reach out for connection with others and I will receive it.

7. Write out a plan of action.

List the steps you will take toward achieving your desired goal. Write down your time frame to begin working on your new contract. Identify what might get in the way and what you will do to get around any difficulties.

8. Evaluate the new contract.

Are you satisfied with your plan? Is there anything you might want to change? When you have followed through, assess your satisfaction with the outcome. Is the whole contract working for you? Is there any piece of it that you need to refine?

By rewriting old contracts and creating new ones, you are charging yourself with new energy. You are renewing and revitalizing your internal power. It was always there, only you hadn't accessed it. With your new contracts, you are creating new sources of inner knowledge. Your new internal agreements will allow you to blossom and to become the person that got lost or left behind.

It has been a long, arduous journey. It has taken much courage on your part to stay on the path. Stay open and keep listening. There is much more to discover and you now have tools to apply to whatever challenges you are confronted with. No more shadows, no more locked doors, no more secrets kept, no more hiding from yourself. It's time to come out into the light. You've earned it and you deserve it.

When you are ready, write your new contract using the following form.

New Contract

I, _____ , commit to the following contract:

Signature: _____ Date: _____

* * * * *

Contract Steps Review

1. Scaling.

2. Write out old contract.

3. Sign commitment statement.

4. Visualize what you want to happen.

5. Write out a contract outline.

6. Write out your new contract using the contract outline.

7. Write out a plan of action.

8. Evaluate the new contract.

Meditation

This is a meditation about completion and acknowledgment. See yourself surrounded with a soft, glowing light. Each breath that you take in brings you a deeper sense of comfort and a feeling of joy. Visualize each cell in your body filling up with light and with love. Acknowledge the hard work you have done. Tell yourself, "I have completed a difficult task. I have moved another step forward in my process of becoming whole and complete within. I am proud of myself and appreciate the opportunity I have given to myself to reach a higher plane of inner knowing and inner growth. I can now allow myself to experience inner peace and inner joy. I am thankful that I have been able to open to my inner guide. I have done a great service to myself."

Learning, Gifts, and Reinforcement

What was it like to write your new contract? What did you struggle with? What was comfortable? How might you approach the process differently next time around? What would you do the same way? Do you feel more empowered? If so, why? If not, what are you still struggling with?

What gifts can you identify as a result of creating a new contract?

If at any point you begin to doubt yourself or your resolve to write a contract, turn inward and ask for guidance. You will be led to the answers you need to hear. If you are not ready, you will hear this. If you are ready, but experiencing some fear, you will know that as well and can use the comforting techniques you have learned to calm and soothe yourself. You don't have to do everything at once. When you are ready, you will do what you need to be doing. Repeat the completion meditation after each contract you create.

Concepts to Remember

1. You can have a more defined sense of self and a clearer vision of what you want and need.

2. Your new contracts will enhance and benefit you.

3. Visualizing is an essential part of the process of creating new contracts. It is fun and empowering.

4. Be reality based.

5. Creating new contracts puts you in charge of the rest of your life.

Chapter 10

The Awakened Self

Evolving through Internal Shifts

How does change occur within? How do you know when you are ready to take the next step? Everyone moves at a different pace. Everyone has their own style and own way of assimilating information. Some people move very quickly because they have been getting ready for a long time on a subconscious level. Others inch along and then suddenly take a huge leap forward. Some people try to rush through change without integrating the information they need to make permanent shifts. And there are those who stay perennially stuck and locked into their patterns.

There is no right way to internal growth, no way that is better than another. Your learning has to do with:

* Your own personal style.

* What you are ready and willing to take in at any one moment.

* What you choose to do with what you have learned.

Internal growth happens through a series of internal shifts. Internal shifts occur when you are ready to incorporate new concepts. You may intellectually understand the meaning of something in your life, but you may be unwilling or unable to integrate what it truly means for you emotionally, psychologically, and spiritually. You will know you are ready for the next step when you are impelled to take that next step. When an internal shift takes places, a knowingness arises within you that won't allow you to stay where you are if where you are is not where you need or want to be. A message gets transmitted through thoughts or feelings that tells you that something needs to change.

This message can transcend fears and negative messages if you allow yourself to trust in it. When you do, you continue your evolutionary process and reach higher levels of awareness. When you don't trust in the message, you remain where you are or slip back to an earlier state of being. This is where all the internal listening work that you have done can serve you well.

Your Real Self

Discovering what you want and what is important for you in this life is your ultimate goal. Wandering unconsciously through life will lead you nowhere in particular. When there is no passion for anything, when life feels dulled and aimless, there is an inner void that must be filled. There is a sense of a lost self that must be found and reawakened. The natural outgrowth of all the work you are doing is to discover your real self.

Discovering who you truly are is your real purpose. You can discover this only when you have cleared away the cobwebs and the clutter that have clouded your vision and your true path. As you remove the veils that have distorted your life view, you will discover your illumined self. Your purest self will evolve and along with that evolution, your real self will appear with amazing brilliance and clarity. You cannot force this to happen. It will occur when you are ready to see with all of your senses and with your whole self. When you are ready, what you need to know will appear, and you will recognize it and accept it.

When you connect to your real self:

* Your life, work, and relationships will flourish.

* You will not question what you are doing and where you are going.

* You will know within the deepest part of yourself what is meaningful and purposeful.

* You will awaken each new day with a sense of vitality and interest, and look forward to what will unfold for you.

The way to your real self is to let go of all judgments about who you think you are and who you think you are expected to be. You are now the one to define who you want to be. Your only limitation will be the thoughts that keep you from believing in yourself. Unless you allow yourself to dream, how do you know how far you can go? Unless you remove all the limiting thoughts and accompanying fears, how can you hope to grasp that which is really within your reach? It is all there to be accessed by you. If you can believe it, you can have it. There are two ways you can choose to live your life. You can stay shut down, or you can open yourself to all the possibilities that there are and allow yourself to receive all the gifts to be given. And then you may celebrate.

Choose Your Own Reality

If you can make a contract to honor yourself, to do most of what you wish to do in your life, to feel self-love and self-compassion, and to end up with as few regrets as possible, then you have lived your life to its fullest. If you do so, you will be uplifted in mind, body, and spirit.

You get to choose your beliefs. You get to formulate your life. That's what this whole book is about. The information presented is only to serve as a guide. You may accept or reject anything that does not feel right for you. Use what works, discard what doesn't. Your truth is for you to decide. Your reality is what you choose it to be, what you want and allow it to be. No one can take that from you ever again.

Your Awakened Self

The self you now choose to be is the self you were meant to be. Your self is glorious, empowered, and ever expanding. Your self has awakened. While this may be exhilarating, this can also present difficulties, because this new self is interconnected with others. As your self awakens, what you see around you may confuse you.

While you may fully embrace and revel in the self you have discovered, you may also feel you are losing an integral piece of this self. What you leave behind, however, may be the debris that has held you to your unhealthy contracts. Releasing your contracts is necessary so that you can regenerate.

In *Women Who Run With the Wolves,* (1997) Clarissa Pinkola Estes presents La Loba, The Wolf Woman. La Loba collects wolf bones and reassembles them. She sings out over the skeleton she is creating and as she does so, a wolf begins to flesh out, comes back to life, and transforms into a laughing woman, running free towards the horizon. I love this story because it so clearly depicts the experience of life, death, and renewal. You have the capacity for renewal. You have the ability, if you so choose, to awaken, to come alive, to flourish, and to be free from constricting contracts.

Your New Territory

Awakening is a rebirth. As you move into your newly evolved self, you see everything around you through a different lens. The way you were and the way you connected with others have changed. You find yourself in new territory as an explorer, where you were once a settler. The landscape appears familiar, yet the details are different. Suddenly, you see what you were unwilling or unable to see before. You become an observer and may find you are less willing to participate in the games and the dramas you were once so entangled and invested in. You may not like what you see and may make choices you would not have had the courage or the will to make prior to this.

Others may also not like what they are seeing and experiencing. You have changed, you are no longer playing by the rules that have been established. This may not feel fair or reasonable. You have pushed the boundaries, broken the contracts, challenged the messages. And while you have succeeded on one front, you may find yourself in conflict on another front.

As you step into your new territory, you open to a reality you have fashioned. No longer unconscious, you are an active participant in the process and progress of your life. You will plant seeds that enable more growth to take place for you and for all those you intersect with. For as you shift, everyone around you must shift as well. And each person you touch in turn touches another, and so on and on, one by one, as you all become cocreators—all of you moving, shifting, and hopefully, awakening.

Living in the Present

You are here, you are now. This one moment is what you have. Regretting yesterday and longing for tomorrow will drain vital energy from you. You cannot have what is lost. You cannot own what does not yet belong to you. Honoring each moment brings you into true inner connection and awareness. With inner connection and awareness, you can more clearly distinguish dissonance within and identify internal contracts that have undermined you.

As an experiment, I decided to pay attention to each moment I could for a whole week. What I learned is that time moves slowly when you focus on the moments. Each act I performed became more meaningful and more pleasurable, because I was attentive to each action. I became more of an actor and less of a reactor in my life. The process of my life was my centralizing theme. Reaching the end goal became less important. When the week was over, I experienced a wonderful feeling of having been *in* my life. I experienced a consciousness and an awareness of each day. I could actually remember what I did on Monday or Wednesday. I never felt I was rushing and doing things just to get them done. By slowing down, I had time to think, to reflect, to make clearer decisions, to connect within and with others in a more peaceful, more real way. When something upset me, I could quickly identify my feelings and connect to the reasons for my reactions, and then could release what I needed to let go of. Try doing this as your own experiment.

Life is replete with distractions, some pleasant, some not. In your very busy, complicated, demanding life, time has a way of barreling forward, and before you know it, the day has passed, the week has escaped you, the month has come and gone, and it's a year later. Living in the present does not mean you have no need to plan for the future. These are not mutually exclusive goals. Planning and visualizing your future are essential if you are to progress in your development.

Being in the present is what will guide you to your future. If you visualize in this moment what you want to happen for you in your future, you can begin to create it. The creation is a process of being very grounded within yourself and very much in touch and in tune with your needs, wishes, and desires. If you avoid the present and live only for the future, you lose a vital component in this creative process. You need to be *in* yourself in order to take that self with you.

Staying grounded, aware, and present takes effort. There is a tendency when something feels uncomfortable to want to ignore it or get away from it. By avoiding the present reality, you are wasting the opportunity to resolve the discomfort—and you may end up carrying it around within you anyway. You'll end up devoting time and energy to something that is really depleting you. Take care of your life now, pay attention, figure it out, resolve what you need to, and then let it go. Staying unconscious is a decision to hide from your life. Living in the present is a choice to:

* See

* Hear

* Feel

* Experience

Changing the course of your life, by identifying, breaking, and rewriting your childhood contracts, can only be accomplished when you live in the present and pay attention to your innermost self.

The Importance of Loving Connections

Your loving connections ground, center, and fulfill you. Material possessions are wonderful and can provide certain kinds of comfort and pleasure. Money can make life a whole lot easier. You can, for example, buy a big, beautiful house and furnish it with expensive antiques, comfortable furniture, and crystal chandeliers. You can also be alone or feel very much alone in that big beautiful house, because in your drive to acquire all these material possessions, you have let go of the loving connections you had. You had no time or energy to put into maintaining them. You forgot. You were unaware that this required effort. You ignored the reality that it would require effort. You thought things would magically work out. And before you knew it, it was too late. And here you sit, alone, not wanting to be alone, in shock that you are alone, and feeling regretful.

This is a scenario to avoid. It does not have to happen. You do not have to be alone. You do not have to be disconnected. You do not have to be without love in your life. Your new, healthy contracts will lead you to healthier and more meaningful connections in your life. All your relationships will be enhanced. Your loving connections consist of the community you draw around you and include your partner, children, parents, siblings, friends, colleagues, pets, neighbors, and of course, yourself.

The number of connections you have is not what is important. What is important is that your connections are real and not based on fulfilling contracts that feed on your need for approval, acceptance, validation, or "what you can do for me." It matters that you are able to reach out and love and are able to accept love in return. And it matters that as you reach out and love, you do this purely and without expectations and demands about what you are supposed to receive in return. And it matters that when you receive love, you give yourself this message:

"I am loved, I am special, and I don't need to do anything other than to accept this gift of love."

The Gift of Laughter

Love lightens your spirit and so does laughter. Laughter has been scientifically proven to affect body chemistry. When you laugh, you release endorphins and that's why it feels so good to laugh. When you laugh, you free your tension and fears and reduce your stress. A good belly laugh is the best thing for your soul. Laughter is a way you can be a child again and be playful. Children love to giggle, love to tell silly jokes to make others giggle. When you are with children, don't you find it easy to play and to giggle and to be silly? But when you go back to the world of adults, don't you become inhibited and stiff and uncomfortable about being silly? Why is this?

The reason is that children are given permission to be child-like. Adults are expected to be adults—serious, reasoning, focused, mature. Being silly and playful is something you are expected to leave behind with your childhood. That's a sad message and agreement to make. You ought not to have to deny yourself something that feels so good to and for you. Laughter is life enhancing and needs to be put on the top of your life to-do list.

Now Congratulate Yourself

Congratulate yourself because you have done something most wonderful. You have:

* Changed your thinking

* Altered your patterns

* Identified, broken, and rewritten your contracts

* Given yourself permission to be who you want to be and to live the life that you want to be living

You are on your path now and you will continue to grow and learn and evolve. You have created a miracle. Now go forth, surround yourself with the gift of laughter and the joy of loving connections.

Meditation

Learn to be in the moment. Take in a slow, deep breath. As you do this, you will take in the moment and your whole body will slow down. As you breathe out, you may release your tension. As you release your tension, your muscles will begin to relax. As your muscles begin to relax, you will feel calmer. As you feel calmer, you will be in touch with your inner feelings and better able to hear your inner voice. As you hear your inner voice, you will be guided to what you need. You may need to cry, you may need to do a release, you may need to acknowledge what you are grateful for, you may need to make a decision about something. As you are guided to what you need, you will experience a sense of inner calm and inner joy as you realize this is the right thing for you. As you experience this inner joy, your soul will glow. As your soul glows, you will touch other souls who will affect still other souls. And all this happened because you took a breath and paid attention to the moment.

Learning, Gifts, and Reinforcement

Assess what you have learned to this point. Where were you in your thoughts, feelings, and relationships when you began this process? What have you found out about the contracts you made in the past and why you made them? Where are you now in terms of your thoughts, feelings, and relationships? What contracts, themes, and patterns have you identified, broken, and rewritten? What have you awakened to? What are the most important concepts you have taken from reading this book? How are things changing? What are you learning about the life you are living now? Where do you still need to grow? Project yourself to age seventy-five and look back on the life you now choose to be living. What do you see? How can you create this life?

Here is a gift from me to you:

You have been traveling for eons, searching out there for something that would fill the void in here. You have worked very hard. You have shown commitment and determination, and this has allowed you to awaken to a self that is filled with self-love. You've brought yourself home. I am so very proud of you. I wish you a joy-filled life.

When you feel you are getting lost, confused, anxious, fearful, angry, frustrated, or anything else that doesn't feel good inside, take a breath in, stop the inner turmoil from increasing, and visualize yourself within a pyramid filled with love.

Concepts to Remember

1. You evolve through internal shifts at your own pace.

2. Discovering who you truly are is your real purpose.

3. Your truth and your reality are what you choose them to be.

4. You have the ability to awaken and to be free from constricting contracts.

5. You will find yourself in a new territory that you have fashioned.

6. Live in the present.

7. Your loving connections ground, center, and fulfill you.

8. Laughter lightens your spirit.

9. Congratulate yourself!

References

Bridges, William. 1980. *Transitions: Making Sense of Life's Changes.* New York: Perseus Publishing.

———. 2001. *The Way of Transition: Embracing Life's Most Difficult Moments.* New York: Perseus Publishing.

Estes, Clarissa Pinkola, Ph.D. 1997. *Women Who Run With the Wolves: Myths and Stories of the Wild Women Archetype.* New York: Ballantine Books.

Fraiberg, Selma H. 1996. *The Magic Years: Understanding and Healing the Problems of Early Childhood.* New York: Simon & Schuster.

Gawain, Shakti. 1978. *Creative Visualization: Meditations.* Novato, Calif.: New World Library.

Moore, Thomas. 1994. *Care of the Soul: A Guide for Cultivating Depth and Sacredness in Everyday Life.* New York: Harper Perennial.

Moyers, Bill. 1993. *Healing and the Mind.* New York: Doubleday.

Muller, Wayne. 1992. *Legacy of the Heart: The Spiritual Advantages of a Painful Childhood.* New York: Simon & Schuster.

Myss, Caroline, Ph.D. 1997. *Anatomy of the Spirit: The Seven Stages of Power and Healing.* New York: Random House.

Peck, M. Scott. 1998. *The Road Less Traveled: A New Psychology of Love, Traditional Values and Spiritual Growth.* New York: Simon & Schuster.

Joan Rubin-Deutsch, LICSW, is a cofounding director of Interactions Counseling and Intervention Center in Littleton, Massachusetts. Ms. Rubin-Deutsch spent two years as Director of the Divorcing Parents workshop, a Massachusetts state-mandated parenting-skills program for divorcing parents. A respected lecturer and workshop leader, she lives in Acton, Massachusetts.

Visit her at http://www.jrdeutsch.com

Some Other
New Harbinger Titles

The Stop Walking on Eggshells Workbook, Item SWEW $18.95

Conquer Your Critical Inner Voice, Item CYIC $15.95

The PTSD Workbook, Item PWK $17.95

Hypnotize Yourself Out of Pain Now!, Item HYOP $14.95

The Depression Workbook, 2nd edition, Item DWR2 $19.95

Beating the Senior Blues, Item YCBS $17.95

Shared Confinement, Item SDCF $15.95

Handbook of Clinical Psychopharmacology for Therpists, 3rd edition, Item HCP3 $55.95

Getting Your Life Back Together When You Have Schizophrenia Item GYLB $14.95

Do-It-Yourself Eye Movement Technique for Emotional Healing, Item DIYE $13.95

Stop the Anger Now, Item SAGN $17.95

The Self-Esteem Workbook, Item SEWB $18.95

The Habit Change Workbook, Item HBCW $19.95

The Memory Workbook, Item MMWB $18.95

The Anxiety & Phobia Workbook, 3rd edition, Item PHO3 $19.95

Beyond Anxiety & Phobia, Item BYAP $19.95

Stop Walking on Eggshells, Item WOE $15.95

The Healing Sorrow Workbook, Item HSW $17.95

The Relaxation & Stress Reduction Workbook, 5th edition, Item RS5 $19.95

Stop Controlling Me!, Item SCM $13.95

The Anger Control Workbook, Item ACWB $17.95

Call **toll free, 1-800-748-6273,** or log on to our online bookstore at **www.newharbinger.com** to order. Have your Visa or Mastercard number ready. Or send a check for the titles you want to New Harbinger Publications, Inc., 5674 Shattuck Ave., Oakland, CA 94609. Include $4.50 for the first book and 75¢ for each additional book, to cover shipping and handling. (California residents please include appropriate sales tax.) Allow two to five weeks for delivery.

Prices subject to change without notice.